PRINT'S BEST LOGOS & SYMBOLS

Copyright © 1990 by RC Publications, Inc.
All rights reserved.
Published by RC Publications, Inc.
104 Fifth Avenue
New York, NY 10011

Manufactured in Hong Kong.

PRINT'S BEST LOGOS & SYMBOLS 2

Library of Congress Catalog Card Number 89-091068
ISBN 09-15734-79-6

RC PUBLICATIONS

President and Publisher: Howard Cadel
Vice President and Editor: Martin Fox
Creative Director: Andrew Kner
Managing Director, Book Projects: Linda Silver
Associate Art Director: Thomas Guarnieri
Administrative Assistant: Nancy Silver
Introduction by: Tom Goss

2

Print's Best
LOGOS & SYMBOLS

WINNING DESIGNS FROM PRINT MAGAZINE'S NATIONAL COMPETITION

Edited by
LINDA SILVER

Art Directed by
ANDREW KNER

Designed by
THOMAS GUARNIERI

Published by
RC PUBLICATIONS, INC.
NEW YORK, NY

INTRODUCTION

This is a book where logos are the stars. In the day-to-day life of graphic communications, logos play a supporting, though essential, role in communication programs. Seldom seen alone, they are applied to other items—letterheads, products, ads—and are always seen in the context of those particular executions. But, as many a designer has discovered, a carefully crafted logo or symbol can be eclipsed by an inappropriate or clumsy application. It is their essential role in graphic communication, then, that makes it worthwhile to examine individual marks both in and out of context.

The roots of what we call the modern logo can be traced back to ancient China when artists and craftsmen marked their work with a distinctive "chop." However, these symbols were pictorial and not abstract ideograms. A blacksmith, for example, might have marked his goods with the image of a horse or anvil, while a cooper might have used the image of a barrel or bucket.

Interestingly, the contemporary manifestations of what has come to be called logo design embrace both approaches, and the 256 logos collected here reflect the wide range of styles and purposes to which logos are now put. Just as logos have come to consist of abstract symbols, letterforms, or illustrations, so too have they come to signify an infinite variety of activities. Where the ancient "chops" identified the work of a particular person, contemporary logos have moved beyond the function of marking the products of individuals and companies to serving as the signature of things as ephemeral as fund-raising events. The ability of logos and symbols to communicate an identity in a single image has made them an ideal tool for a range of applications. Included in this book are logos designed for companies and individual entrepreneurs, but also for one-time events and other ephemera. One of the more

CONTENTS

interesting of these is a logo for a student working on a Masters degree, the purposes being to create a distinct identity for herself as an eager graduate student and to gain the cooperation of her research subjects.

But what exactly is a logo if it can be so many things and be used for so many purposes? In the end, there is really only one test, and that is that the image, symbol, or arrangement of letterforms must be legally copyrightable. Initials set in Helvetica Bold, or any other face, do not in and of themselves constitute a logo. Beyond that, it becomes an issue of good design and here we come to the purpose of this, and the other books in the *PRINT's Best* series. The work presented here has been selected from that already published in recent editions of PRINT's Regional Design Annual, a comprehensive collection of superior design chosen by the editors and art director of PRINT magazine.

The purposes of the Regional Design Annual and the *PRINT's Best* books are complementary. Where the Annual seeks to show as much good work from around the country as possible, the *PRINT's Best* books endeavor to highlight a particular category of graphic design and give it a detailed and generous showing. In the case of logos and symbols, this means that the individual mark is reproduced larger than life—often larger than its use in the actual application. Examples of such applications are included in this book where available. No attempt has been made to arrange the work shown in arbitrary categories, but rather to present these superior marks in a manner calculated both to give pleasure and stir the imagination. Given the venerable pedigree of logos and symbols, it will come as no surprise to find that, as far as imagery and devices are concerned, designers appear to be mining the same vein. But it is the original use of old themes that distinguishes the work presented here and makes this a valuable treasury and reference source.—*Tom Goss*

Twelve Californias

department store promotion.

DESIGN FIRM: Design Guys,

Minneapolis, Minnesota

ART DIRECTOR:

Robert Valentine/

Bloomingdale's

DESIGNER: Steven Sikora

ILLUSTRATORS:

Steven Sikora, Gary Patch

Bloomingdale's

BLOOMINGDALES
TWELVE CALIFORNIAS

LOS ANGELES

THE NORTH COAST

THE CENTRAL VALLEY

SHASTA CASCADE

SAN DIEGO

THE HIGH SIERRA

ORANGE COUNTY

THE DESERTS

THE GOLD COUNTRY

SHASTA CASCADE

SAN FRANCISCO

THE INLAND EMPIRE

A guide to schools for the
learning disabled.
DESIGN FIRM: Crocker, Inc.,
Boston, Massachusetts
ART DIRECTOR/
DESIGNER: Bruce Crocker
DESIGNER: Annette Rapier

DESIGN FIRM:

Communicā, Inc., Toledo, Ohio

AGENCY:

Marketing Communications

Group

DESIGNER/ILLUSTRATOR:

Jeff Kimble

Sauder Farm/Craft Village/Barn Restaurant

Bachner & Co.

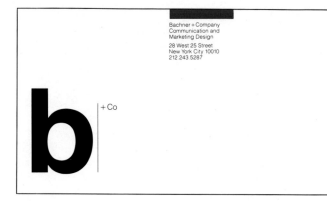

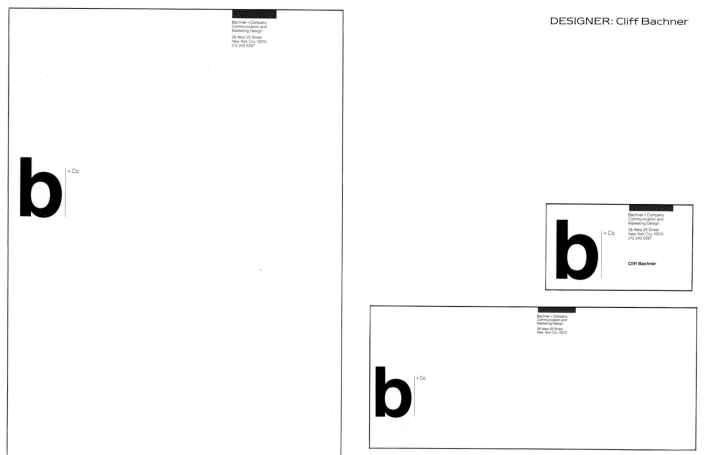

DESIGN FIRM:

Bachner & Co., New York,

New York

DESIGNER: Cliff Bachner

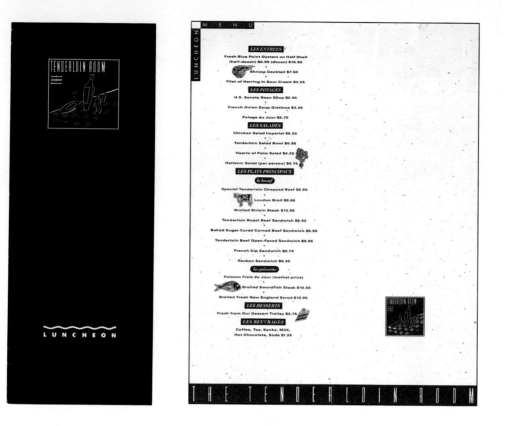

TENDERLOIN ROOM
THE

DESIGN FIRM:

The Idea Department,

St. Louis, Missouri

ART DIRECTOR:

Maris Cirulis

DESIGNER/ILLUSTRATOR:

Jennifer Anderson

fishbone

DESIGNER/ILLUSTRATOR:

Barry Fitzgerald,

Tonawanda, New York

CLIENT: United University

Activities Board, University

of Buffalo

DESIGNER: Michael Maselli,

West Haverstraw,

New York

Blue Swann Dry Cleaners

10

Annual conference held in
Cincinnati.

DESIGN FIRM: E Design,

Cincinnati, Ohio

DESIGNER: Ellen Lytle

University & College Designers Association

DESIGN FIRM:

Rusty Kay & Associates,

Santa Monica, California

ART DIRECTOR: Rusty Kay

DESIGNER/ILLUSTRATOR:

Susan Rogers

Fish Co. (Seafood Restaurant)

The Institute for Limb Preservation

DESIGN FIRM:

Gullickson Illustration

Design, Denver, Colorado

DESIGNER/ILLUSTRATOR:

Vicki Gullickson

AGENCY:

Mickey Musset Advertising

INSTITUTE FOR LIMB PRESERVATION
™
Jody S. Dillavou, R. N.
Clinical Director

1721 E. 19th Ave., Suite 210 Denver, CO 80218
303-832-LIMB   1-800-262-LIMB

A team approach to limb salvage for cancer, trauma, infection, and replantation.

Dayton Hudson (Department Store Promotions)

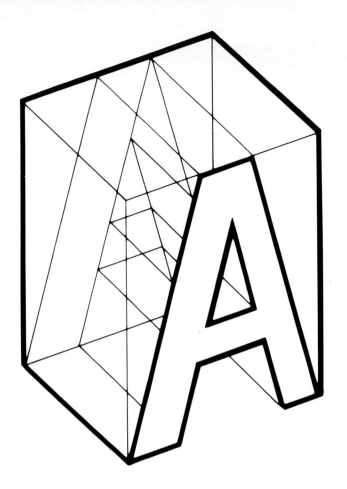

CHANGING
P·A·R·A·D·I·G·M·S
our strategy for the
90'S

S U N W E S T

DESIGN FIRM:

Dwight Douthit Design,

Houston, Texas

ART DIRECTOR:

Robin Mueller

DESIGNER: Dwight Douthit

ILLUSTRATOR:

Rubén Esparza

CLIENT: Lexford Properties

Cholewa & Associates Inc   501 West Lake Street   suite 208   Elmhurst   Illinois   60126   312 834 9466   Fax 312 834 0475

A commercial art and

production studio.

DESIGN FIRM:

Bluebirdesign,

Oak Brook, Illinois

ART DIRECTOR:

James Cholewa

DESIGNER: George Frenoy

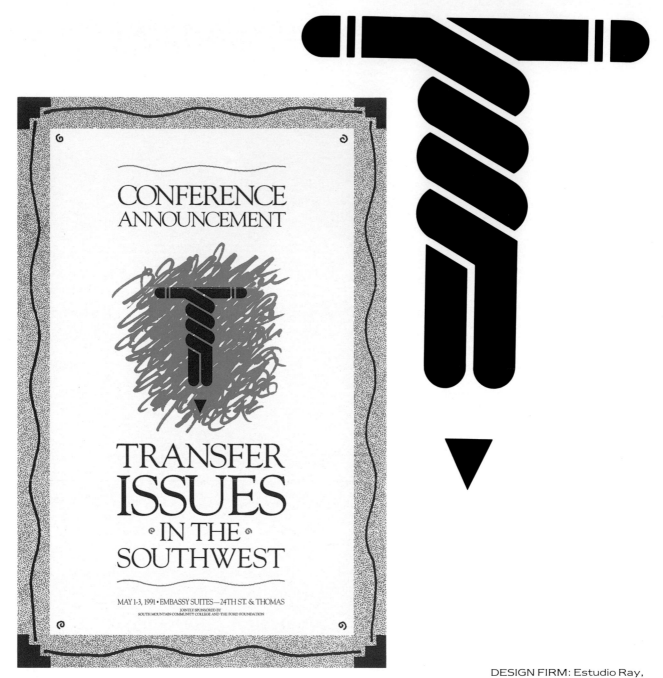

Transfer Issues in the Southwest (Education Conference)

DESIGN FIRM: Estudio Ray, Phoenix, Arizona

ART DIRECTORS/ DESIGNERS:

Christine Ray, Joe Ray

CLIENT: South Mountain Community College

OFFICE PRODUCTS

DESIGN FIRM:

Krawczyk Design, Inc.,

Orlando, Florida

DESIGNER: Joe Krawczyk

Bailey Office Products

Mary Kay Cosmetics 25th Anniversary

DESIGN FIRM:

Sibley/Peteet Design,

Dallas, Texas

DESIGNER: Rex Peteet

T H A T ' S   R I T C H
D I N I N G   +   D A N C I N G

DESIGN FIRM:

Michael Patrick Partners,

Palo Alto, California

DESIGNER/ILLUSTRATOR:

Scott Brown

Motto

A company which

represents home

furnishings manufacturers.

DESIGN FIRM:

Paul Curtin Design,

San Francisco

ART DIRECTOR: Paul Curtin

DESIGNER: Robin Terra

18

DESIGN FIRM:

Hampden-Sydney College

Publications, Hampden-

Sydney, Virginia

DESIGNER:

Richard McClintock

CLIENT:

Rose Bower Vineyards

Grand Tetons or Bust

A women's art direction

symposium.

DESIGN FIRM: Tharp Did It,

Los Gatos, California

DESIGNER: Rick Tharp

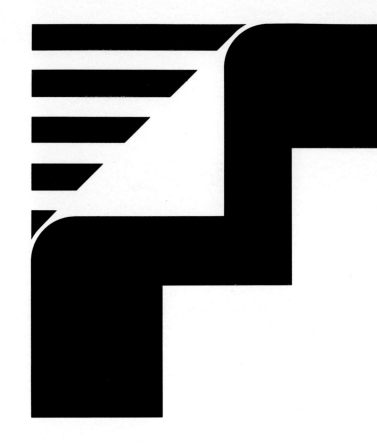

Fraser Paper Co.

DESIGN FIRM:

SmithGroup, Inc., Portland,

Oregon

ART DIRECTOR:

Thom Smith

DESIGNER:

Gregg Frederickson

Entrekin Zucco Advertising

DESIGN FIRM:

Frank D'Astolfo Design,

New York, New York

DESIGNER: Frank D'Astolfo

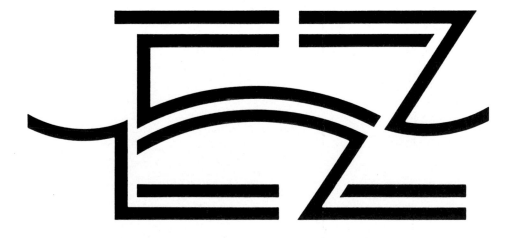

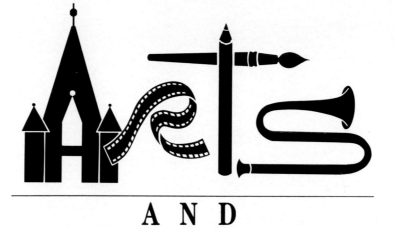

DESIGN FIRM:

Cats Pajamas, St. Paul,

Minnesota

ART DIRECTOR:

Mike Hazard

DESIGNER: Patricia Olson

Arts & Eats (St. Paul Downtown Council Culture & Restaurant Promotion)

DESIGN FIRM:

Hornall Anderson Design

Works, Inc., Seattle,

Washington

DESIGNERS: John Hornall,

Jack Anderson

ILLUSTRATORS:

Brian O'Neill, Jack Anderson

Hornall Anderson Design Works

Discover
the Difference...
Cold Smoked
Hawaiian Ahi

It's Tuna!
As you've never tasted it before
"A delicious alternative in smoked fish"
Chef Jean Marie Josselin, Owner Pacific Cafe
Winner of the American Seafood Challenge

For information
call your favorite
supplier or the
State of Hawaii
Ocean Resources Branch
(808) 548-6262
FAX (808) 523-8637

Hawaii Seafood
PO Box 2359
Honolulu, Hawaii 96804
Circle Reader Inquiry #33

Fresh from Hawaii

Hawaii Seafood (State Promotional Campaign)

Fresh from Hawaii

DESIGN FIRM:

Eric Woo Design, Honolulu,

Hawaii

DESIGNER: Eric Woo

CALLIGRAPHER: Jack Elder

Fresh from Hawaii

Hawaii Seafood

DESIGN FIRM:

Clement Mok designs, Inc.,

San Francisco, California

DESIGNER: Clement Mok

CONNECT

Humana, Inc. (Hospital/Medical Center Group)

DESIGN FIRM:

Design Continuum,

Dayton, Ohio

DESIGNER: John Emery

DESIGN COORDINATOR:

Jerry Lee Holt/Humana, Inc.

DESIGN FIRM:

B. Luce Graphics, Riverside,

Connecticut

DESIGNER:

Barbara B. Luce

Barbara B. Luce

B. Luce Graphics
90 Winthrop Drive
Riverside, CT 06878
Phone: (203) 637-0553

B. Luce Graphics
90 Winthrop Drive
Riverside, CT 06878

B. Luce Graphics
90 Winthrop Drive
Riverside, CT 06878
Phone: (203) 637-0553

DESIGN FIRM:

Newman Design

Associates, Guilford,

Connecticut

DESIGNER/ILLUSTRATOR:

Bob Newman

Michael Gomez Public Relations

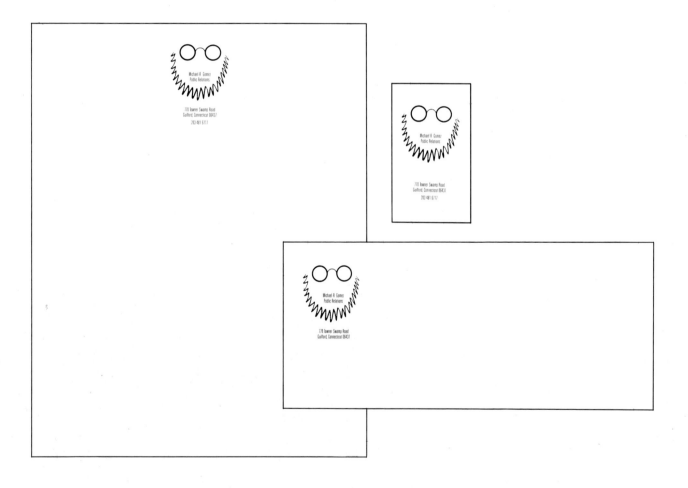

A+

Annual high school exhibit at
the Arlington Arts Center.
DESIGN FIRM:
Konetzka Design Group,
Washington, DC
DESIGNER:
Michael Konetzka

Washington State University Track & Field Team

DESIGN FIRM:

Bryan Friel Design, Long

Beach, California
DESIGNER: Bryan Friel

DESIGNER: Joe Pinciotti,

Toledo, Ohio

Waiter Race for United Way

San Francisco Tuba Quartet

DESIGN FIRM:

Philip Quinn & Partners,

Redwood City, California

DESIGNER: Philip Quinn

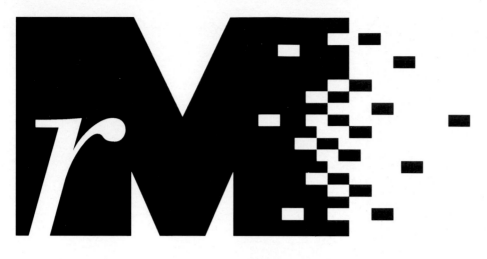

Rochester **Monotype**

Rochester Monotype (Typesetting & Computer Graphics)

360 North Street
P.O. Box 1169
Rochester, New York 14603

716-546-1690

Patricia C. Corcoran
Marketing Director

DESIGN FIRM:

Dunn and Rice Design,

Rochester, New York

DESIGNER: John Dunn

ZOHRA
SPA & BODY CLINIQUE

DESIGN FIRM: Ross Design,

Wilmington, Delaware

DESIGNER: Tony Ross

ILLUSTRATOR:

Conrad Velasco

Houston Tenneco Marathon

DESIGN FIRM:

Hanagriff/King Design, Inc.,

Houston, Texas

ART DIRECTORS:

Ron Hanagriff, Fred King

DESIGNER/ILLUSTRATOR:

Fred King

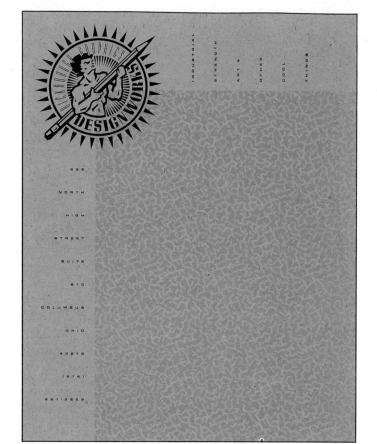

DESIGN FIRM:

Rickabaugh Graphics,

Gahanna, Ohio

ART DIRECTOR/

DESIGNER: Eric Rickabaugh

ARTIST: Tony Meuser

Designworks (Retail Products)

DESIGN FIRM:

Cowell Design Group,

Burbank, California

ART DIRECTOR: Lee Cowell

DESIGNER: Kevin Weinman

West Construction

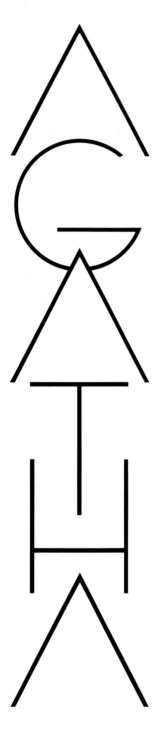

DESIGN FIRM:

Johnson & Simpson,

Newark, New Jersey

DESIGNER: Joe Katz

Agatha at the Strand (Women's Clothing Store)

DESIGN FIRM: 2 Designers

DESIGNERS:

Jeannine Channin, Wendy

Mure, New York, New York

ILLUSTRATOR:

Susan Vaughn

Down Under (Restaurant)

32

DESIGN FIRM:

Sibley/Peteet Design,

Dallas, Texas

DESIGNER/ILLUSTRATOR:

Rex Peteet

Mesa (Retail Store)

Billy Goat Strut Publishing

DESIGN FIRM:

Lauder Creative Services,

Louisville, Kentucky

DESIGNER: Sheryl Lauder

BILLY GOAT STRUT
PUBLISHING, INC.

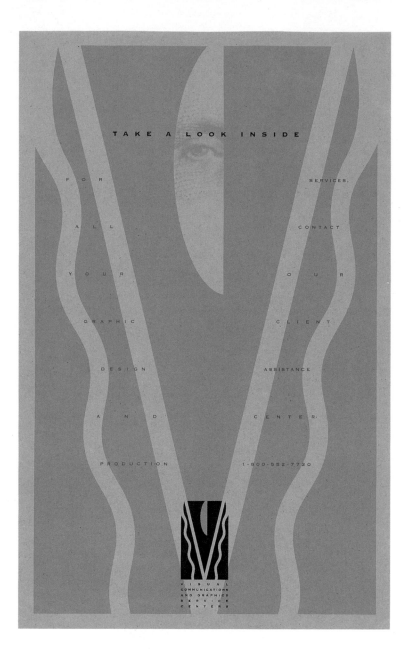

TAKE A LOOK INSIDE

FOR   SERVICES,

ALL   CONTACT

YOUR   OUR

GRAPHIC   CLIENT

DESIGN   ASSISTANCE

AND   CENTER

PRODUCTION   1-800-552-7720

VISUAL
COMMUNICATIONS
AND GRAPHICS
SERVICE
CENTERS

DESIGN FIRM:

AT&T Visual Communications,

Parsippany, New Jersey

DESIGNER: Terry J. Keenan

AT&T Visual Communications (Internal Corporate Design Group)

CLOWES MEMORIAL HALL
OF BUTLER UNIVERSITY

DESIGN FIRM:

Dean Johnson Design,

Indianapolis, Indiana

DESIGNER/ILLUSTRATOR:

Scott Johnson

Clowes Memorial Hall (Performing Arts Theater)

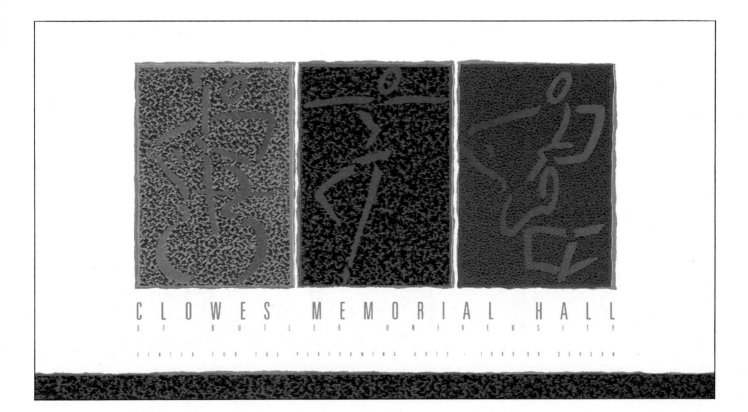

CLOWES MEMORIAL HALL
OF BUTLER UNIVERSITY
CENTER FOR THE PERFORMING ARTS · 1989-90 SEASON

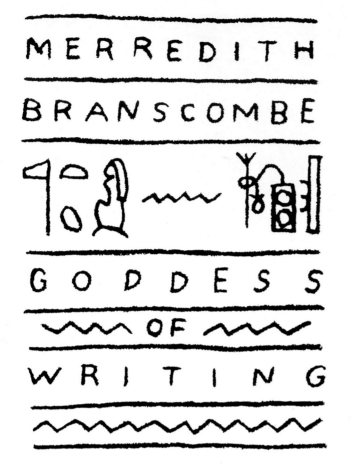

Merredith Branscombe

DESIGN FIRM:

Hamilton & Associates

Advertising, Denver,

Colorado

DESIGNER: Michelle Torrez

Singles Society (Christian Singles Bible Study & Ministry)

DESIGN FIRM:

Art Thou Art?, Pomona,

California

DESIGNER: Jerry Price

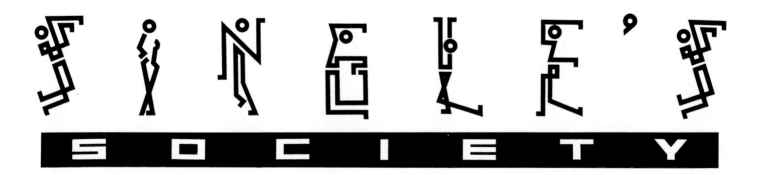

DESIGN FIRM:

Genuine Graphics,

Lake Oswego, Oregon

DESIGNER: Mike Virosteck

DESIGN FIRM: Barnstorm,

Atlanta, Georgia

DESIGNER: Ted Fabella

Birdsong Family Reunion 1990

37

C L A S S I C

C A R

L O F T

of

Westchester, Ltd.

A classic and collectable car storage and sales facility.

DESIGN FIRM:

The Design Office, Inc., New York, New York

DESIGNERS:

Joseph Feigenbaum, Elizabeth Castagna

DESIGN FIRM:

Richards & Swensen, Inc., Salt Lake City, Utah

ART DIRECTOR/

DESIGNER:

Micheal Richards

Cold Fusion Institute (University of Utah Research Facility)

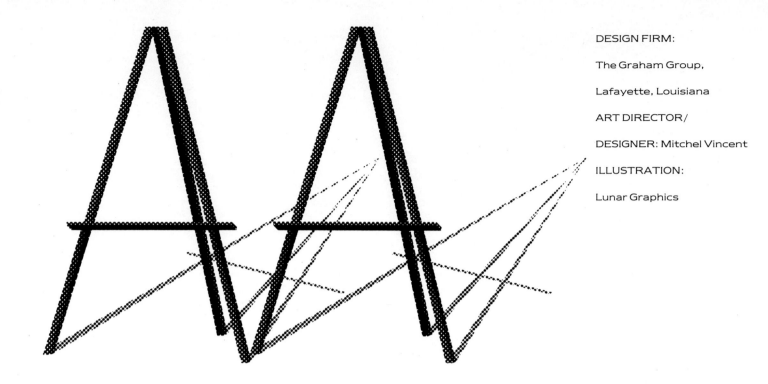

DESIGN FIRM:

The Graham Group,

Lafayette, Louisiana

ART DIRECTOR/

DESIGNER: Mitchel Vincent

ILLUSTRATION:

Lunar Graphics

Artist's Alliance (Fine Artists Group)

GEORGIA ARTISTS

DESIGN FIRM:

The Visual Design Center,

Georgia State University,

Atlanta, Georgia

ART DIRECTOR:

Jeff A. McGinnis

DESIGNER: Walt Griffin

CLIENT:

Dekalb Council for the Arts

Georgia Artists (Exhibition)

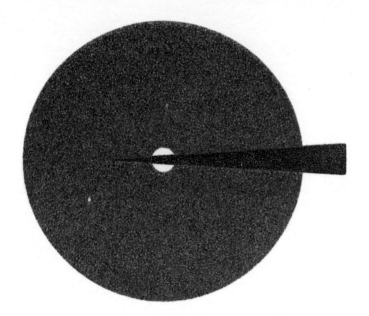

Cymbal Crown (Cymbal Design/Manufacture)

DESIGN FIRM:

The Bradford Lawton

Design Group, San Antonio,

Texas

ART DIRECTORS:

Ellen Pullen, Bradford

Lawton

DESIGNER:

Bradford Lawton

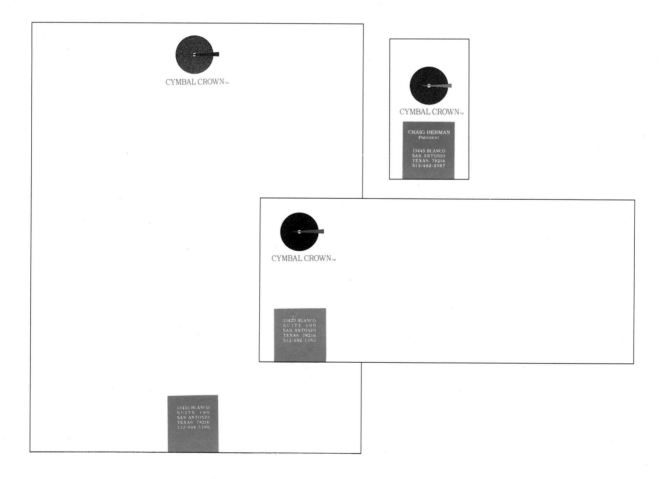

DESIGN FIRM:

Shannon & Shannon,

Holland, Michigan

DESIGNER: Amy Leppert

CLIENT: Jean Pluta

Handwoven (Handweaver)

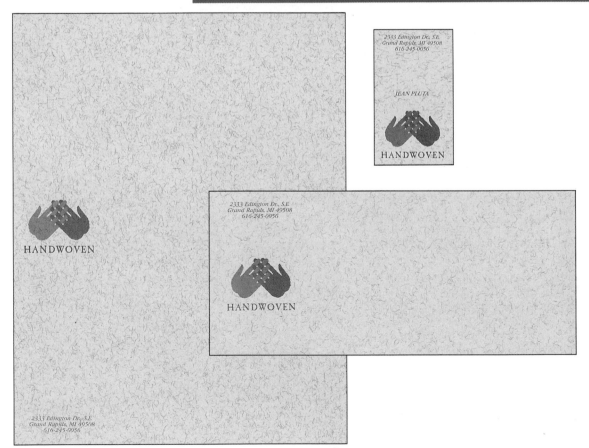

Guadalupe Learning Center

DESIGN FIRM:

Estudio Ray, Phoenix,

Arizona

ART DIRECTORS/

DESIGNERS: Christine Ray,

Joe Ray

ILLUSTRATOR: Christine Ray

DESIGN FIRM:

Victoria Miller Design,

Los Angeles, California

ART DIRECTORS:

Victoria Miller, Jeffrey

Spear

DESIGNER: Victoria Miller

National Restaurant Association

DESIGN FIRM:

Shauck Design, Columbia,

Maryland

ART DIRECTOR/

DESIGNER: Chuck Shauck

COOL CLEAR WATER

4237 BRIGHT BAY WAY
ELLICOTT CITY, MARYLAND 21043

Cool Clear Water (Water Purification Specialists)

WAT.E.R. (WATersafety Education Resource)

A non-profit organization

committed to reducing the

number of infant drownings.

DESIGN FIRM:

Morgan & Co., Phoenix,

Arizona

ART DIRECTOR:

David Morgan

DESIGNER/ILLUSTRATOR:

Terry Richards

E.Cecchi Farms

E. Cecchi Farms (Roadside Vegetable Stand)

DESIGN FIRM: DRC Design,

Feeding Hills, Massachusetts

DESIGNER: David Cecchi

ILLUSTRATOR:

Linda Schiwall-Gallo

PRINTER: ES Sports (Apron)

Our annuals are perennial favorites.

And our perennials are pretty popular, too! Whether you're looking for annuals, perennials, vegetable plants or shrubs, we've got everything you need.

Rose bushes, clematis, potting soil, peat moss, and more: all you need in the garden this Spring is right here.

The stand is now open with our own hothouse tomatoes and field fresh lettuce, native asparagus and spinach, and a wide selection of fresh fruits and vegetables, eggs, and more!

E.Cecchi Farms
1109 Springfield Street, Feeding Hills, Massachusetts 01030

DESIGN FIRM:

Horjus Design/Illustration,

San Diego, California

DESIGNER/ILLUSTRATOR:

Peter E. Horjus

Zia's (Restaurant)

DESIGN FIRM:

The Bradford Lawton

Design Group, San Antonio,

Texas

ART DIRECTORS:

Bradford Lawton, Jody

Laney

DESIGNER:

Bradford Lawton

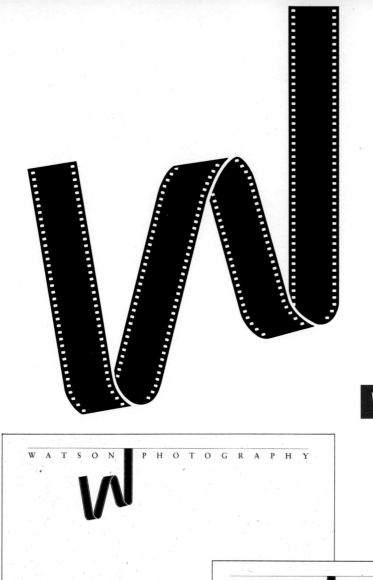

DESIGN FIRM:

Rickabaugh Graphics,

Gahanna, Ohio

ART DIRECTORS:

Eric Rickabaugh, Mark Krumel

DESIGNER/ILLUSTRATOR:

Mark Krumel

Watson Photography

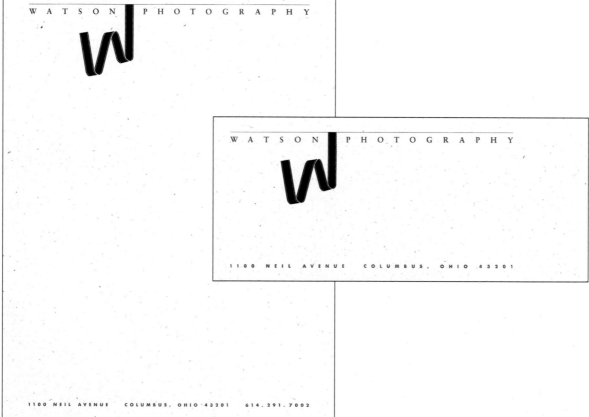

W A T S O N   P H O T O G R A P H Y

1100 NEIL AVENUE   COLUMBUS, OHIO 43201   614.291.7002

W A T S O N   P H O T O G R A P H Y

1100 NEIL AVENUE   COLUMBUS, OHIO 43201

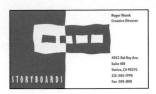

STORYBOARDS

STORYBOARDS

Storyboards, Inc.

A firm representing
storyboard artists in the
advertising and film industries.
DESIGN FIRM:
Vrontikis Design Office
Los Angeles, California
ART DIRECTOR:
Petrula Vrontikis
DESIGNER: Bob Dinetz

STORYBOARDS

4052 Del Rey Ave.

Suite 108

Venice, CA 90292

213-305-1998

Fax: 305-1810

STORYBOARDS

4052 Del Rey Ave.
Suite 108
Venice, CA 90292
213-305-1998
Fax: 305 1810

DATE:

TO:

INVOICE #

ATTENTION:
ART DIRECTOR:
CLIENT:
P.O. # / JOB #:

DESCRIPTION OF JOB:

STORYBOARDS

4052 Del Rey Ave. Suite 108
Venice, CA 90292

TAX:

TOTAL:

TERMS: TOTAL DUE ON PRESENTATION OF INVOICE / PLEASE MAKE CHECK PAYABLE TO STORYBOARDS, INC.

SAVE THE RAINFOREST.

DESIGN FIRM:

Hal Riney & Partners,

San Francisco, California

DESIGNER: Chris Chaffin

ILLUSTRATOR: Michael Bull

Save the Rainforest (Non-Profit Organization)

We've gone to great lengths to get your attention.

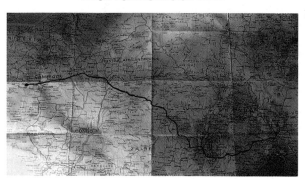

(The route Tempe Thompson, Zoi Cohen and Nelson Hoffman took, cycling through the African Rainforest.)

The thing we heard most of all was that it couldn't be done. But we also knew it was all we really could do. We weren't rich. We weren't rock or movie stars whose names bring instant press to the issue.

We were just two guys and a gal. And all we had to offer was time. And energy. And a crazy idea.

Raise awareness for the African Rainforest by riding across it.

Fortunately, the Bicycle Exchange of Cambridge and Merlin Mountain Bikes didn't think we were

completely nuts, and offered us equipment. And since Adventure Center Travel along with Sabena World Airlines were nice enough to come up with some tickets, and Ricoh with cameras, in March of last year, we set off.

Five months and 2,500 miles of mud roads, foot paths and elephant trails later (only 100 miles of paved road), we made it.

Enough can't be said about the beauty of the Rainforest. But there are writers much more poetic than us, that can talk about that. Enough

also can't be said about the destruction (25,000 acres a day).

Because once we stop talking about it, once we stop keeping it top-of-mind, once we stop worrying, it will stop being.

And somehow, that's what we must stop from happening.

If you want to help save the African Rainforest, contact (or make check payable to) Rainforest Action Network/Africa, P.O. Box 637, Charleston, MA 02129. Your contribution is tax-deductible.

(Our thanks to Outside Magazine for running this ad.)

IT WILL NOT BE YOU, BUT THESE EIGHT MEN, WHO WILL DECIDE THE FATE OF YOUR CHILDREN.

EVERY DAY, we hear something new about the vital significance of the rainforest to the future well-being of our planet.

News stories describe the crucial role it plays in supplying the world with water and oxygen. Medical experts tell us about the recently-discovered, cancer-curing properties of its indigenous plantlife. Scientists explain the unique defense it provides against the "Greenhouse Effect," which may already be raising the earth's temperature to dangerous new levels.

We also hear that this irreplaceable ecosystem is being destroyed at the alarming rate of 75,000 acres a day. And we fear for the future of our planet. And our children.

And yet, all too often, we feel powerless to do anything about it.

The same, however, cannot be said of the eight men pictured above. In the next few months, these men will determine future actions on three separate fronts that, together, significantly affect not only the rainforest, but, ultimately, what kind of world future generations will inherit.

It is important that we understand the issues they face. And equally important that they know what we think about those issues. While there is still time.

I. WORLD BANK LOAN TO BRAZIL.

The World Bank is presently arranging a series of loans to Brazil for up to $500 million. When the loan was originally proposed, much of the funding was slotted for the building of over 50 dams. If these dams are built, 15 million acres of rainforest will be mapped under water forever.

Earlier this year, public opinion (much of it from U.S. taxpayers, the largest contributors to the World Bank) forced postponement of this proposal. At this time, it appears that the loan might well become reality. What hasn't yet been resolved is whether or not the dams will be built, or how many.

Four of the men pictured above will wield considerable influence on what happens next. They include World Bank President Barber Conable and Brazilian President Jose Sarney, as well as President George Bush and Secretary of Treasury Nicholas Brady, who not only determine our country's vote, but set the tone for many others as well. Voting on the final loan proposal could easily take place within the next few months, if not sooner.

II. THE PENAN RAINFOREST OF BORNEO.

The island of Borneo is divided into two countries which, together, share the vast Penan Rainforest.

In Malaysia, that rainforest is being destroyed, literally almost overnight, by a burgeoning logging industry. The Penan tribespeople, among the last hunter-gatherer societies left on the planet, have bodily blockaded logging trucks. But the Malaysian government is arresting the protesters, and Japan continues to import 60% of the forest's yield, in the face of over thousands of letters of protest from its own citizens.

In Indonesia, the Penan Rainforest is also being systematically stripped, at the rate of hundreds of trees a day. The raw timber is then converted to plywood and shipped to lumber companies in the United States.

Three of the men pictured above have great influence on the future of the Penan Rainforest. They are Shinroku Morohashi, President of Mitsubishi Corporation, one of the largest Japanese importers of Penan timber; T. Marshall Hahn Jr., Chairman and CEO of Georgia-Pacific Corporation, the principal importer of Penan plywood to the United States; and the Malaysian Chief Minister of Sarawak, YAB Patinggi Haji Abdul Taib Mahmud.

In a similar situation in Thailand, after the loss of much of their rainforest, a total ban on logging was enacted earlier this year. Without the same kind of ban in Borneo, the Penan Rainforest will almost certainly disappear within five years.

III. THE SCOTT PAPER COMPANY.

In the near future, this American-based company is planning to convert over 2,000,000 acres of Indonesian rainforest into a pulp and woodchip plantation for the manufacture of paper products. Future plans reportedly include a similar project in Papua New Guinea.

The loss of this rainforest, like all rainforests, will be irreversible. In this case, at least 21,000 tribespeople — people who for centuries have relied on the rainforest for survival — will also lose their only home and way of life.

One of the gentlemen pictured above, Scott Paper CEO Philip Lippincott, will have great influence on how this project is finally enacted.

At present, Scott Paper Company says the final decision is two years away, but it has already established the first nursery for seedlings that would replace the existing forest. Concurrently, it has begun negotiations for an imported work force and machinery. An area of rainforest larger than Delaware hangs in the balance.

Between them, the eight men pictured above share the awesome responsibility of determining the future of much of the remaining rainforest on earth, and, consequently, the future of our planet and children.

Between all of us, we share the responsibility of expressing our opinions of what should happen next. And so, we urge you to write these men and speak your mind now.

We recognize that they find themselves under enormous pressure, facing the most complex and delicate of situations. But as men of reason and intelligence, they will listen.

And, at this important time, they deserve nothing less than full knowledge of what you think.

For more information about participation in and contributions to the battle to save our rainforests, please contact:

Save The Rainforest/
Rainforest Action Network,
301 Broadway, Suite A,
San Francisco, CA 94133

1. BARBER CONABLE, President, World Bank, 1818 H Street N.W. Washington, D.C. 20433.
2. NICHOLAS F. BRADY, Secretary of Treasury, U.S. Treasury Department, 1500 Pennsylvania Ave. N.W. Washington, D.C. 20220.
3. PRESIDENTE JOSE SARNEY, Presidencia da Republica, Gabinete Civil, Placio do Planalto, 70150 Brasila-DF, Brasil.
4. GEORGE BUSH, President, The White House, 1600 Pennsylvania Ave. N.W. Washington D.C. 20500.
5. YAB DATUK PATINGGI HAJI ABDUL TAIB MAHMUD, Chief Minister of Sarawak, and Minister of Resource Planning, Chief Minister's Office, Petra Jaya, Kuching Sarawak, Malaysia.
6. PHILIP LIPPINCOTT, Chief Executive Officer, Scott Paper Company, 1 Scott Plaza, Philadelphia, PA 19113.
7. SHINROKU MOROHASHI, President and Director, Mitsubishi Corporation, 6-3 Marunouchi 2-chome, Chiyoda-ku, Tokyo 100-86.
8. T. MARSHALL HAHN JR., Chairman and CEO, Georgia-Pacific Corporation, 133 Peachtree St. N.E. 51st Floor, Atlanta, GA 30303.

ZANE

DESIGN FIRM:

Bechlen/Gonzalez, Inc.,

Honolulu, Hawaii

DESIGNER: Leo Gonzalez

RSP

RSP
Diane Trout-Dertei

RSP Architects Ltd.
120 First Avenue North
Minneapolis, MN 55401
FAX 612 • 339 • 6760
612 • 339 • 0313

RSP

Alexander F. Ritter, A.I.A.
Michael J. Plautz, A.I.A.

Dick B. Daniels, A.I.A.
Jim Fitzhugh, A.I.A.
Robert M. Lucius, A.I.A.
Dennis L. Mulvey, A.I.A.
David C. Norback, A.I.A.

RSP Architects Ltd.
120 First Avenue North
Minneapolis, MN 55401
FAX 612 • 339 • 6760
612 • 339 • 0313

RSP Architects

DESIGN FIRM:

Little & Company,

Minneapolis, Minnesota

CREATIVE DIRECTOR:

Monica Little

ART DIRECTOR:

Paul Wharton

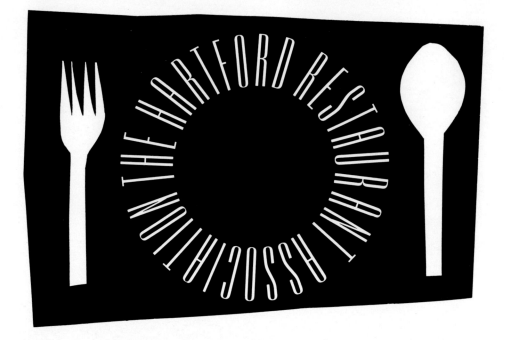

DESIGN FIRM:

Dennis Russo Design,

Hartford, Connecticut

ART DIRECTOR:

Dennis Russo

DESIGNER:

Maria Fatima Mota

Hartford Restaurant Association

THE

HARTFORD

RESTAURANT

ASSOCIATION

221

MAIN

STREET

HARTFORD

CONNECTICUT

06106

203.525.8200

THE
HARTFORD
RESTAURANT
ASSOCIATION
221
MAIN
STREET
HARTFORD
CONNECTICUT
06106
203.525.8200

THE

HARTFORD

RESTAURANT

ASSOCIATION

221

MAIN

STREET

HARTFORD

CONNECTICUT

06106

Summer Foods Demonstration

Joyce Goldstein Summer Foods Demonstration
RESERVATION FORM

(Please Print)

Name (Last, First, Initial)

Street/P.O. Box

City   State   Zip

(   )   (   )
Home Telephone   Work Telephone

☐ Yes, I/We wish to attend the Joyce Goldstein
Summer Foods Demonstration on Tuesday, July 12.
Please reserve _____ seats at $35 per person.
Reserve by Thursday July 7, 1988.
☐ I/We cannot attend the Summer Foods
Demonstration but wish to contribute $_____.
Enclosed is my check for $ _____ made payable
to the San Francisco Hillel. Please detach and mail
to: San Francisco Hillel
        33 Banbury Drive
        San Francisco, CA 94132

For additional information call 333-4922

A food tasting event.

DESIGN FIRM:

Kaptur Design, Lakewood,

Ohio

DESIGNER: Kurt Kaptur

CLIENT: S.F. Hillel

SIZZLE INTO SUMMER

with the
Joyce Goldstein
Summer Foods
Demonstration
and Tasting!

designed by kurt kaptur

Date:

Tuesday, July 12

Place:

Caffe Quadro
180 Pacific Avenue Mall
(between Pacific & Front Street)
San Francisco

Time:

6:00 - 6:30 pm - Wine & Pizza
6:30 - 7:30 pm Summer Foods Demonstration
begins promptly
7:30 - 8:00 pm Summer Foods Tasting

Cost:

$35 Per Person - Please reserve by Thursday, July 7

◆ Your donation is a tax deductible
contribution to the San Francisco Hillel.

◆ Joyce Goldstein, Chef and Owner of Square One
and Caffe Quadro in San Francisco, is also a food writer,
restaurant consultant and kitchen designer.

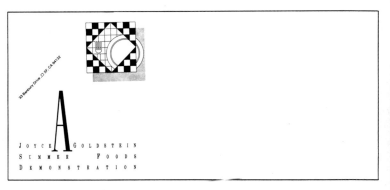

33 Banbury Drive ☐ SF, CA 94132

A

JOYCE GOLDSTEIN
SUMMER FOODS
DEMONSTRATION

51

DESIGN FIRM:

Vance Wright Adams

Associates, Pittsburgh,

Pennsylvania

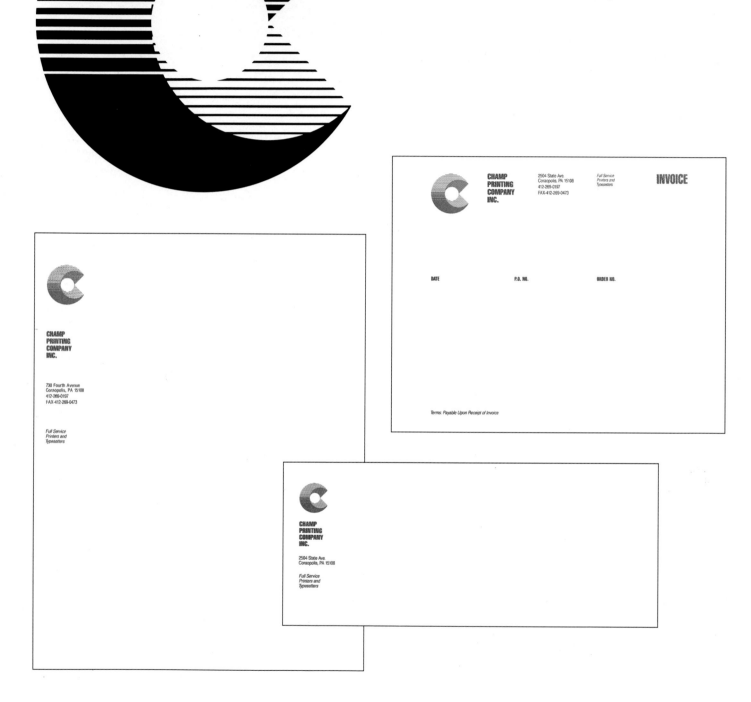

CHAMP
PRINTING
COMPANY
INC.

2504 State Ave.
Coraopolis, PA 15108
412-269-0197
FAX-412-269-0473

Full Service
Printers and
Typesetters

INVOICE

DATE   P.O. NO.   ORDER NO.

Terms: Payable Upon Receipt of Invoice

CHAMP
PRINTING
COMPANY
INC.

730 Fourth Avenue
Coraopolis, PA 15108
412-269-0197
FAX-412-269-0473

Full Service
Printers and
Typesetters

CHAMP
PRINTING
COMPANY
INC.

2504 State Ave.
Coraopolis, PA 15108

Full Service
Printers and
Typesetters

52

DESIGN FIRM:

Michael Orr & Associates,

Inc., Corning, New York

ART DIRECTOR/

DESIGNER: Michael Orr

DESIGNER: Michael Callahan

CLIENT:

Corning Incorporated

Industrial Products Division

Finspångs Företag (Consulting)

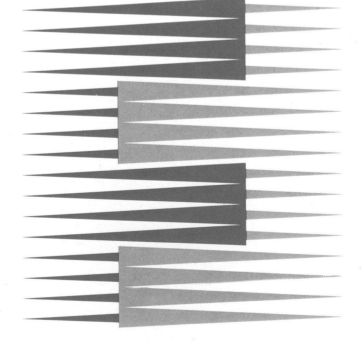

DESIGN FIRM:

Arnell Design, Inc., Sterling,

Virginia

ART DIRECTOR/

DESIGNER:

Kymberly Arnell

DESIGN FIRM:

Joseph Dieter Visual

Communications,

Baltimore, Maryland

DESIGNER:

Joseph M. Dieter, Jr.

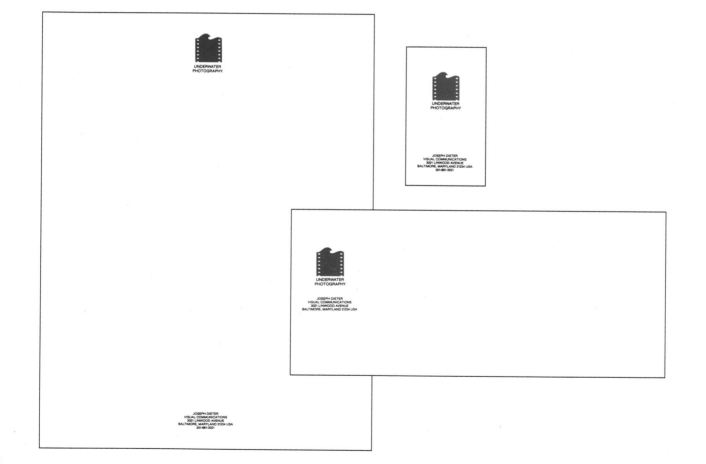

UNDERWATER
PHOTOGRAPHY

JOSEPH DIETER
VISUAL COMMUNICATIONS
3021 LINWOOD AVENUE
BALTIMORE, MARYLAND 21234 USA
301-661-3021

DESIGN FIRM: IDEAS,

San Francisco, California

ART DIRECTOR:

Robin Brandes

DESIGNERS: Calvin Hom,

Sharon Lee

Shearwater (Residential/Commercial Waterfront Development)

395 Oyster Point Blvd., Suite 405   South San Francisco, CA 94080   415.266.9080   FAX 415.266.8930

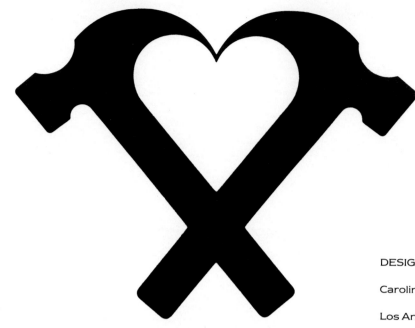

DESIGNER:

Caroline Misner,

Los Angeles, California

Integrity Construction

A walking/running

promotional event.

DESIGN FIRM:

Evans/Spangler Design,

Seattle, Washington

DESIGNER: Curtis Asplund

Seattle Ad Federation

A firm providing benefit and

risk management services.

DESIGN FIRM:

Rickabaugh Graphics,

Gahanna, Ohio

ART DIRECTOR/

DESIGNER: Eric Rickabaugh

Frank Gates Service Company

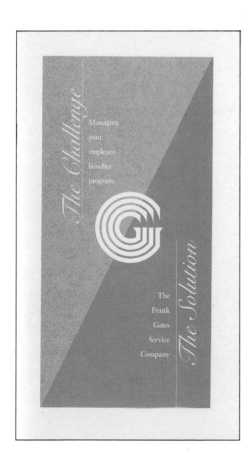

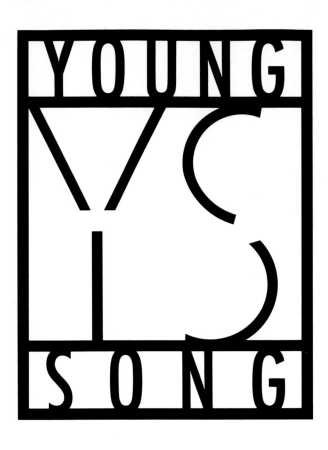

DESIGN FIRM:

Bruce Yelaska Design,

San Francisco, California

DESIGNER: Bruce Yelaska

Young Song (Women's Apparel Manufacturer)

DESIGN FIRM:

Michael Stanard, Inc.,

Evanston, Illinois

ART DIRECTORS:

Marcos Chavez, Mark Naden

DESIGNER: Marcos Chavez

DESIGN FIRM:

Hornall Anderson Design

Works, Inc., Seattle,

Washington

ART DIRECTOR:

Jack Anderson

DESIGNERS:

Jack Anderson, Mary

Hermes, David Bates

ILLUSTRATOR: David Bates

CLIENT:

Consolidated Restaurants

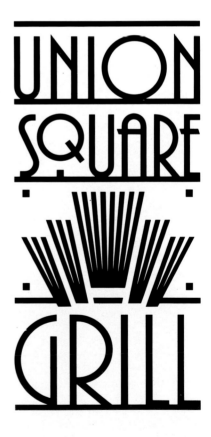

Union Square Grill

The Dynamic Duo Studio (Illustration)

DESIGN FIRM:

The Dynamic Duo Studio,

New York, New York

DESIGNERS/ILLUSTRATORS:

Arlen Schumer, Sherri

Wolfgang

Frank's Pizza & Stromboli

DESIGN FIRM:

Mike Harper Design,

Sterling, Virginia

DESIGNER: Mike Harper

Dreyer's Food Service

DESIGN FIRM:

Michael Osborne Design,

San Francisco, California

DESIGNER:

Michael Osborne

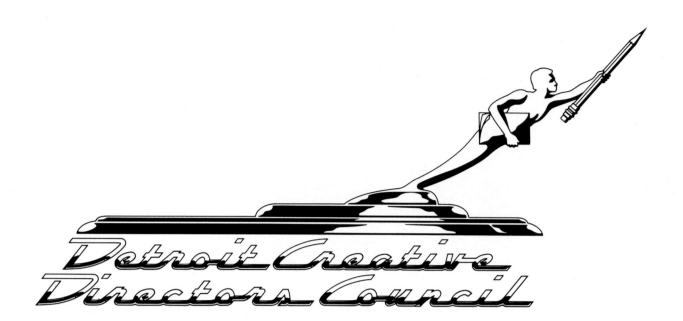

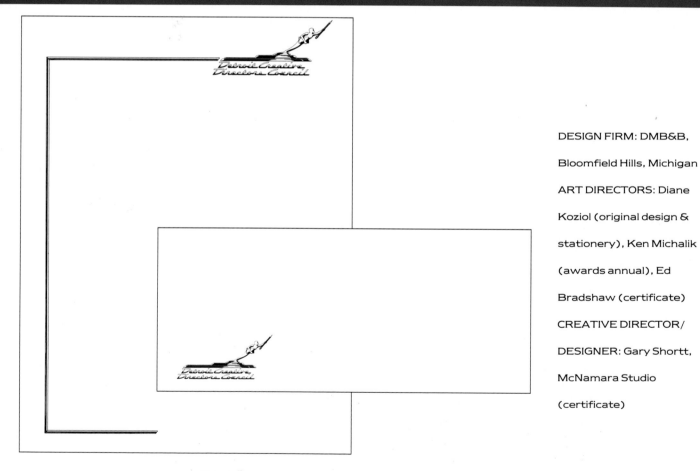

DESIGN FIRM: DMB&B,

Bloomfield Hills, Michigan

ART DIRECTORS: Diane

Koziol (original design &

stationery), Ken Michalik

(awards annual), Ed

Bradshaw (certificate)

CREATIVE DIRECTOR/

DESIGNER: Gary Shortt,

McNamara Studio

(certificate)

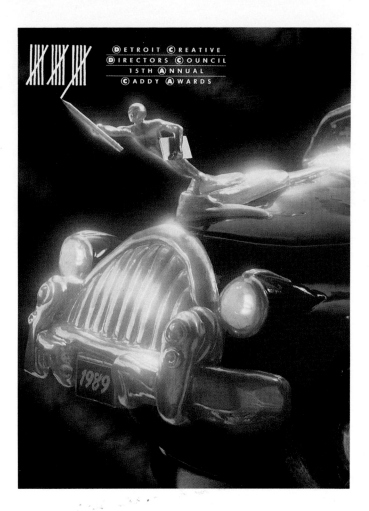

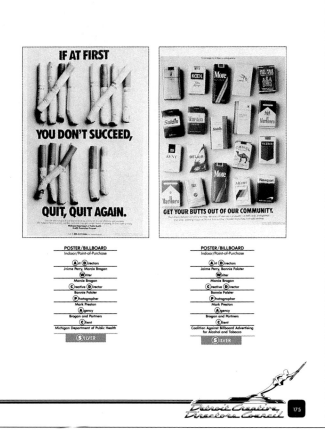

ILLUSTRATOR: Ann Redner

(original design & stationery)

LETTERER:

Bruno Hohmann (original

design & stationery)

PHOTOGRAPHER:

Steve Petrovich (awards

annual)

HOOD ORNAMENT MODEL:

Acme Special Effects

(awards annual)

One Smart Cookie (Cookie Store)

DESIGN FIRM:

Sullivan Perkins, Dallas,

Texas

ART DIRECTOR:

Ron Sullivan

DESIGNERS: Diana McKnight,

Max Wright

ARTIST: Diana McKnight

God's Country

Title logo used for Oregon

Shakespeare Festival

production of a play about

white supremacists in the

U.S.

DESIGN FIRM:

Ken Parkhurst &

Associates, Los Angeles,

California

ART DIRECTOR:

Ken Parkhurst

DESIGNER:

Denis Parkhurst

PUBLICATIONS DIRECTOR:

Hilary Tate

Tee Shirt Co.

DESIGN FIRM:

Knoth & Meads, San Diego,

California

DESIGNER: José Serrano

ILLUSTRATOR: Dan Thoner

DESIGN FIRM:

Tow & Tow Design, Vernon,

Connecticut

DESIGNERS: Jennifer Tow,

David Tow

ILLUSTRATOR: David Tow

Chester Village Bed & Breakfast

Our home is now open to guests as the Chester Village Bed & Breakfast. With its airy, comfortable rooms, reading nooks and sunny porches, it is meant to be a refreshing and relaxing retreat for travellers and businesspeople.

We have five guest rooms available, three with private baths, and two which share a bathroom. These two rooms may become a suite, if you wish.

Gracious breakfasts may be enjoyed each morning in the dining room, on the veranda or in the sunroom. Later, you may have an informal afternoon tea, or sip tall lemonades.

Located in a friendly New England town with a storybook village center boasting fine antique, gift and artisan shops, Chester Village Bed & Breakfast is a recently renovated home with an open door to travellers and visitors to the Connecticut River Valley.

AREA ATTRACTIONS

The Connecticut River Valley is humming with activities year-round. A stone's throw away is the ferry and Gillette Castle, Essex Steam Railroad, the Florence Griswold Historical Museum, the Goodspeed Opera House, Ivoryton Playhouse, art galleries and river cruises. Additionally, there are local events, such as the Deep River Fife and Drum Muster and productions by the National Theater of the Deaf, housed right in Chester. Mystic Village and Marine Life Aquarium are a short excursion, as is the U.S. Naval Submarine base in Groton.

A pleasant day can be had antiquing, hiking, picnicing, and boating. There are several fine lakes and beaches in the area. Just ask us about the area's state parks and trails. Or you can just sit on the veranda in our wicker rocker and enjoy the scenery, sounds and scents that have nourished painters, writers, musicians and sculptors for over a hundred years.

Chester is the perfect for a romantic weekend away. Some of the area's est dining is provided in nearby villages, includin Chester's own Restaurar Village and Fiddler's (sea A finer night cannot be h than to stroll down to th village heart to dine or d into shops, and wander b up to Chester Village Be Breakfast under a canopy starlight, anytime of the

For a truly relaxing retre leave your car behind, as amenities are within str distance of the inn.

Please ask us if you wo like assistance in planni activities, or if you have special requests. We're h to ensure your enjoymer

For reservations, call:
203 526-9770.
Come stay with us!

Your hosts,
**Thayer & Michael
Quoos-Momparler**

Convention of the American
College of Cardiology.

DESIGN FIRM:

Johnson Design Group, Inc.,

Falls Church, Virginia

ART DIRECTOR:

Len Johnson

DESIGNER:

Tom Gamertsfelder

ACC '91 Atlanta

Poverty Level Records (Record Company Label)

DESIGN FIRM:

Paula Fortney & Associates,

Chicago, Illinois

DESIGNER:

Scott Dempsey Smith

BIYOSHI

1965 HUNTINGTON DR. ALHAMBRA CA 91801
818 458 1979

DESIGNER:

Katherine Miura Wong

COMPUTER ARTIST:

Guy Kalicicki

BIYOSHI

1965 HUNTINGTON DR. ALHAMBRA CA 91801
818 458 1979

DATE			STYLIST

CLIENT			PHONE

SERVICE	PRICE
☐ HAIRCUT	
☐ BLOWDRY	
☐ COLOR	
☐ HIGHLIGHTS	
☐ PERMANENT	
☐ CONDITIONER	
☐ _____	
☐ _____	
SUBTOTAL	
TOTAL	

☐ CASH   ☐ CHECK   ☐ CHARGE   ☐ NO CHARGE

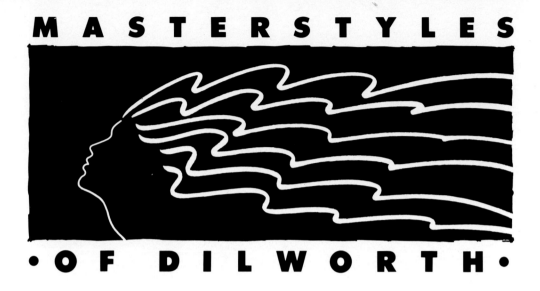

DESIGN FIRM

The Owens Agency,

Charlotte, North Carolina

DESIGNER: Bill Owens

Romantically Yours

A store that sells romantic

accessories.

DESIGN FIRM:

Sommese Design, State

College, Pennsylvania

ART DIRECTOR: Carl Mill

DESIGNER/ILLUSTRATOR:

Kristin Sommese

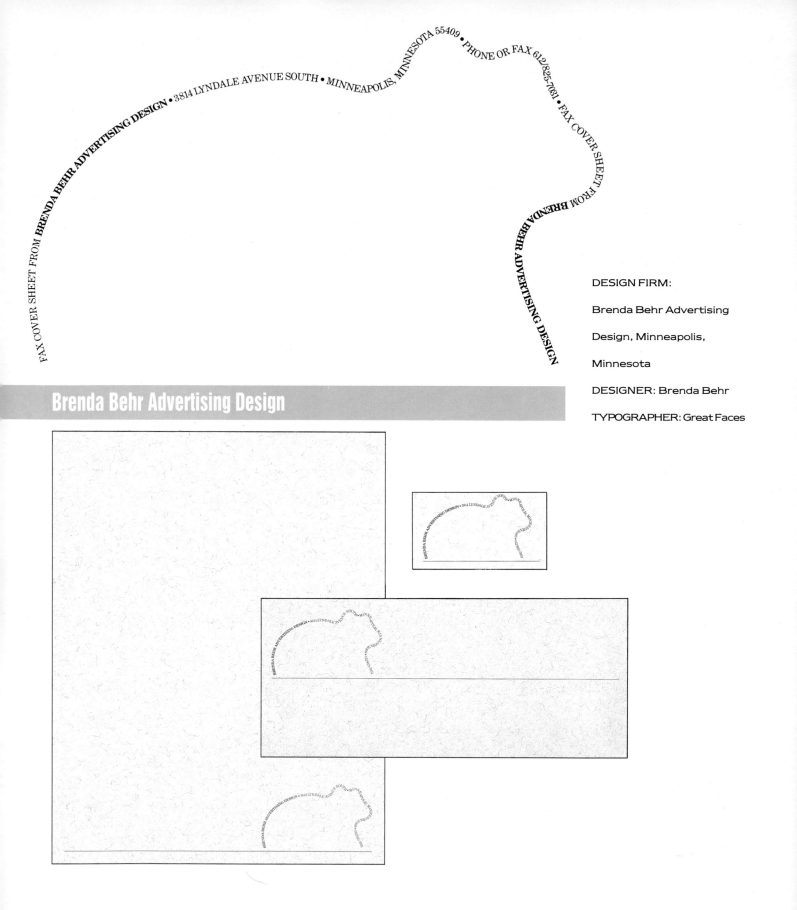

FAX COVER SHEET FROM **BRENDA BEHR ADVERTISING DESIGN** • 3814 LYNDALE AVENUE SOUTH • MINNEAPOLIS, MINNESOTA 55409 • PHONE OR FAX 612/825-7681 • FAX COVER SHEET FROM **BRENDA BEHR ADVERTISING DESIGN**

Brenda Behr Advertising Design

DESIGN FIRM:

Brenda Behr Advertising

Design, Minneapolis,

Minnesota

DESIGNER: Brenda Behr

TYPOGRAPHER: Great Faces

DESIGN FIRM:

Design Farm, New York,

New York

DESIGNER: Jay Sylvester

Design Farm

298 MULBERRY ST
SUITE 7K
NEW YORK NY
1 0 0 1 2
212 334 8178

PURCHASE ORDER

DATE

TO

FROM

PROJECT

DELIVERY INSTRUCTIONS

ITEM   QUANTITY

ORDERED BY

298 MULBERRY ST 7K NEW YORK NY 10012 TEL/FAX 212 334 8178

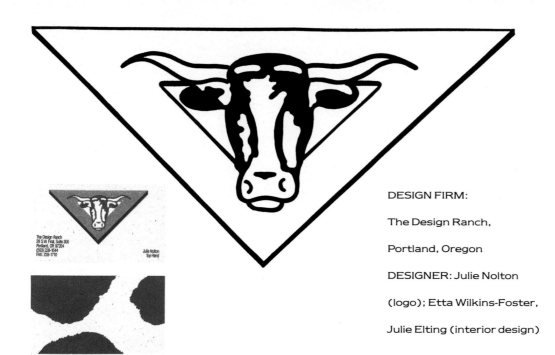

DESIGN FIRM:

The Design Ranch,

Portland, Oregon

DESIGNER: Julie Nolton

(logo); Etta Wilkins-Foster,

Julie Elting (interior design)

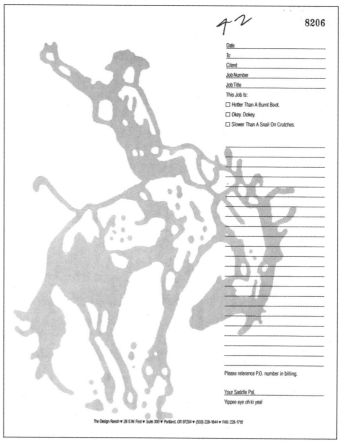

8206

Date
To
Client
Job Number
Job Title
This Job Is:
☐ Hotter Than A Burnt Boot.
☐ Okey. Dokey.
☐ Slower Than A Snail On Crutches.

Please reference P.O. number in billing.

Your Saddle Pal,
Yippee eye oh ki yea!

The Design Ranch ♥ 28 S.W. First ♥ Suite 300 ♥ Portland, OR 97204 ♥ (503) 228-1644 ♥ FAX: 228-1710

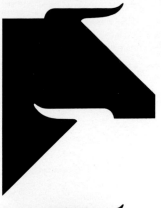

ART DIRECTOR/

DESIGNER:

Stephen Kalibatas,

Minneapolis, Minnesota

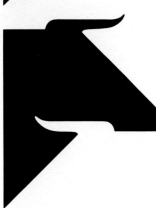

EASTERN BREEDERS

A service providing in-home

care for sick children.

DESIGN FIRM:

Bellin Hospital, Green Bay,

Wisconsin

DESIGNER/ILLUSTRATOR:

Dan Green

CLIENT:

Patricia A. Cooksey/

Bellin Hospital/

Bellin Home Care Services

Bellin Tender Bear Child Care

DESIGNER/ILLUSTRATOR:

Jim Lambrenos, Atco,

New Jersey

Jim Lambrenos (Illustrator)

DESIGN FIRM:

Kiku Obata & Co., St. Louis,

Missouri

CREATIVE DIRECTOR:

Kiku Obata

DESIGNER: Richard Nelson

Run for Reading (St. Louis Public Library Fundraiser)

DESIGN FIRM:

Patrick Soohoo Designers,

Los Angeles, California

ART DIRECTOR:

Patrick Soohoo

DESIGNER: Katherine Lam

AGENCY: HDM

Los Cabos (Mexico) Tourism Board

LOS·CABOS

M I R R E X™

Mirrex (Truck Ornaments)

DESIGN FIRM:

SBG Partners,

San Francisco, California

ART DIRECTOR:

Courtney Reeser

DESIGNER: Jackie Foshaug

PROGRAM DIRECTOR:

Jeffrey Ivarson

ACCOUNT DIRECTOR:

Susie Wright

CLIENT: Paccar Parts

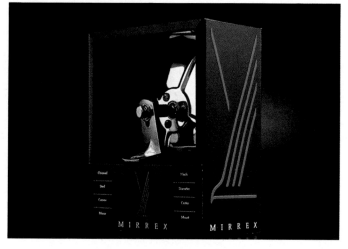

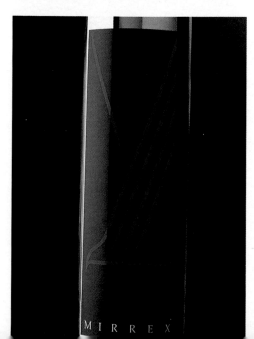

R Ō T I

DESIGN FIRM:

Arias + Sarraille, Palo Alto,

California

ART DIRECTOR:

Mauricio Arias

DESIGNER:

Catherine Richards

CLIENT: Pacific Union Hotel

Rōti (Restaurant)

Connecticut College

DESIGN FIRM:

Ted Bertz Design, Inc.,

Middletown, Connecticut

DESIGNER: Ted Bertz

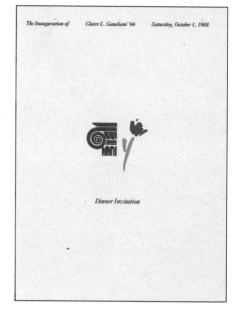

The Resort at Squaw Creek (Conference Resort)

DESIGNER:

Melanie Doherty,

San Francisco, California

ILLUSTRATOR:

Anthony Russo

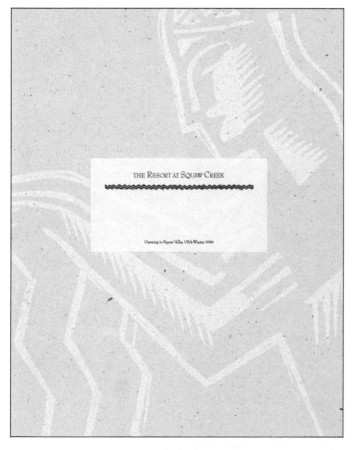

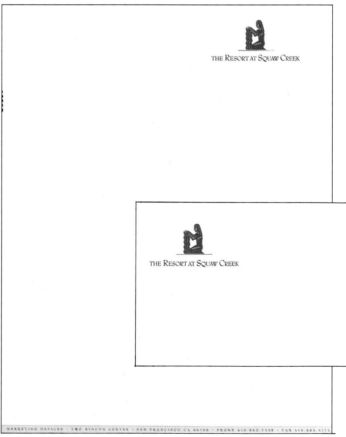

NED

NATIONAL ENTERTAINMENT DATA

DESIGN FIRM:

Rod Brown Design,

Richardson, Texas

DESIGNER/ILLUSTRATOR:

Rod Brown

National Entertainment Data (Talent Representative)

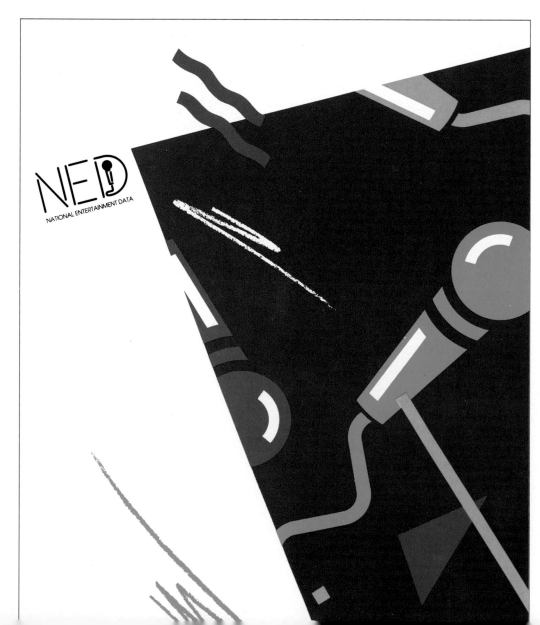

ILLUSTRATOR:

Rob Saunders, Boston,

Massachusetts

ART DIRECTOR:

Richard Reed/State Street

Marketing Communications

DESIGNER: Carol Doherty

CLIENT: State Street Bank

Webb's Coffee (Refreshment Service)

DESIGN FIRM:

Image Design, Nashville,

Tennessee

DESIGNER: Howard Diehl

ILLUSTRATOR:

Robert Froedge

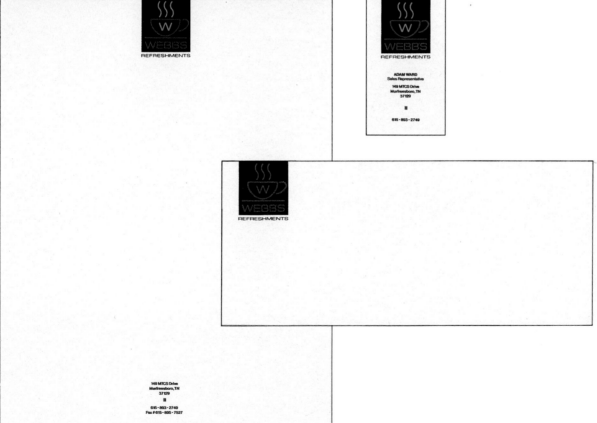

A non-profit program

providing hot meals to the

homebound elderly.

DESIGN FIRM:

Ostro Design, Hartford,

Connecticut

ART DIRECTOR/

DESIGNER/ILLUSTRATOR:

Michael Ostro

Meals on Wheels

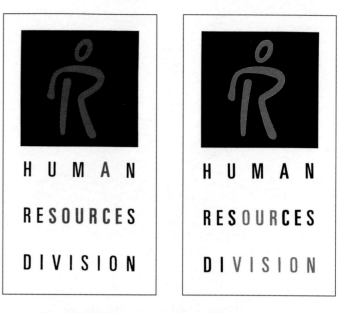

H U M A N

RESOURCES

DIVISION

H U M A N

RESOURCES

DIVISION

Human Resources Division of Corning

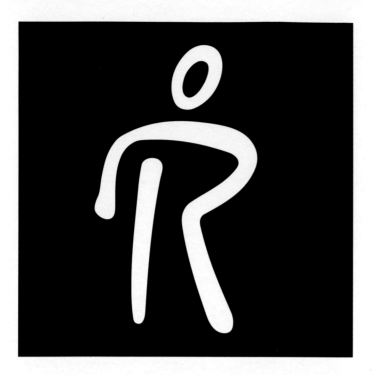

1990 Quarterly Recognition

The Greenville Plant requested tools for Career Planning. With very little notice, Julie Sommers installed Careerpoint in the plant, trained a coordinator and organized support materials for the software user. Julie's quick response allowed the HR Division to respond to an unexpected opportunity with a quality solution. Julie's error-free performance met Greenville's requirements and is indicative of her ongoing commitment to quality.

Julie Sommers

is hereby awarded this certificate

by the Human Resources Division

of Corning Incorporated

for outstanding performance in

the Total Quality Program.

Richard C. Marks

Sr. Vice President
Human Resources Division

CORNING

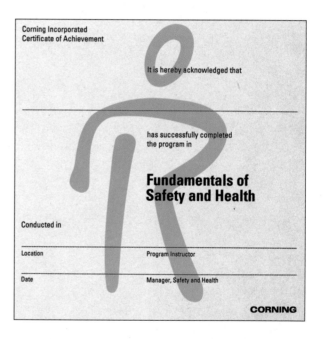

Corning Incorporated
Certificate of Achievement

It is hereby acknowledged that

_____

has successfully completed
the program in

Fundamentals of Safety and Health

Conducted in

Location _____ Program Instructor _____

Date _____ Manager, Safety and Health _____

CORNING

Dick Marks would like you to
join him for a special policy
meeting on Thursday, May 17, 1990
from 8:00 a.m. to 10:00 a.m. in the
Glass Center large auditorium.

CORNING

Thank You!

Ŕ H U M A N R E S O U R C E S
D I V I S I O N Ŕ H U M A N R
E S O U R C E S D I V I S I O
N Ŕ H U M A N R E S O U R C E
S D I V I S I O N Ŕ H U M A N
R E S O U R C E S D I V I S I
O N Ŕ H U M A N R E S O U R C
E S D I V I S I O N Ŕ H U M A
N R E S O U R C E S D I V I S
I O N Ŕ H U M A N R E S O U R
C E S D I V I S I O N Ŕ H U M
A N R E S O U R C E S D I V I
S I O N Ŕ H U M A N R E S O U
R C E S D I V I S I O N Ŕ H U
M A N R E S O U R C E S D I V
I S I O N Ŕ H U M A N R E S O
U R C E S D I V I S I O N Ŕ H
U M A N R E S O U R C E S D I
V I S I O N Ŕ H U M A N R E S
O U R C E S D I V I S I O N Ŕ

CORNING

ART DIRECTOR:

Frederick Murrell/Corning

Incorporated, Corning,

New York

DESIGNERS:

Rodney Reynolds (symbol

& collateral material);

Douglas Harp, Michelle

Lockwood, William Lucas,

Frederick Murrell,

(collateral materials)

DESIGN FIRM:

Sullivan Perkins, Dallas, Texas

ART DIRECTOR/

DESIGNER/ILLUSTRATOR:

Jon Flaming

COPYWRITER: Scott Simmons

DESIGN FIRM:

Bruce Yelaska Design,

San Francisco

ART DIRECTORS:

Bruce Yelaska, Anne Fox

DESIGNER/ILLUSTRATOR:

Bruce Yelaska

CLIENT:

McKesson Corporation

Taking Care of Business (Sales Program)

HEARTS · HAMMERS

A neighborhood

revitalization group.

DESIGN FIRM: RBMM,

Dallas, Texas

DESIGNER: Dick Mitchell

ILLUSTRATORS:

Victoria Clary, Tami Motley

Heart of America Northwest

A non-profit citizens

awareness/action group.

DESIGNER:

Shaun Hubbard, Seattle,

Washington

MEADOWGATE

MEADOWGATE

A Rental Community.

Warm and welcoming Meadowgate is designed to make you feel thoroughly at home ▪ Each roomy, cheerful apartment is filled with features to make life more pleasant ▪ Like ample kitchens with oak cabinetry, dishwashers — even microwave ovens ▪ And large private patios and balconies that bring the natural beauty of trees and flowers indoors ▪ Outside, you'll find more than an acre of green gardens, with a pool, spa, playground and pleasant quiet corners for relaxing under the trees ▪ Discover a different kind of apartment living ▪ Make Meadowgate your home ▪

DESIGN FIRM:

Josh Freeman/Associates,

Los Angeles, California

ART DIRECTORS:

Josh Freeman, Vickie

Sawyer Karten

LETTERER: Bob Maile

CLIENT:

Community Dynamics

GA

Type Selection

Graphic Access, Inc.

475 Commonwealth Avenue

Boston, MA 02215

Telephone 617 262 8829

Modem 617 262 5864

Fax 617 262 4921

GA

Graphic Access, Inc.

475 Commonwealth Avenue

Boston, MA 02215

Telephone 617 262 8829

Modem 617 262 5864

Fax 617 262 4921

Here is some information about Graphic Access, the hippest service bureau in town. As you read through these sheets, you will see that we have high resolution output, film capabilities, color output, self service stat camera and other related equipment. But machines are only a part of the picture. What sets us apart is our service.

Everything at Graphic Access has been designed to furnish our customers with the finest service. We have two imagesetters, allowing us to offer high quality output while-you-wait (at no additional cost) and speedy turn arounds on your super rush jobs. Our spacious office provides a comfortable and relaxing work environment, or if you prefer to stay where you are, we can receive your files via modem. With over 750 typefaces, we have the font you need. And we are happy to provide you with any screen fonts you want, just bring in a disk. The staff at Graphic Access is friendly, patient, and most importantly, knowledgeable. Trained in both computers and design, we can answer both technical and aesthetic questions with confidence, and a smile.

If you have any questions, don't hesitate to call. We are looking forward to speaking with you and doing business with you.

Graphic Access (Service Bureau)

DESIGN FIRM:

Graphic Access, Boston,

Massachusetts

DESIGNER: Amy Diamond

GA

DESIGN FIRM:

Stan Gellman Graphic

Design, Inc., St. Louis,

Missouri

DESIGNER: Stan Gellman

FX | **MICHAEL FOX, INC.** | *Architects*
Interior Consultants
Planners

100 South Fourth Street   Suite 700
St. Louis, Missouri 63102
314 621 4343

Michael Fox, Inc. (Architects & Interior Consultants)

Duree Residence   *Residential Addition*   *New Construction*
O'Fallon, Illinois

MICHAEL FOX, INC. | *Architects*
Interior Consultants
Planners

MICHAEL FOX, INC. | *Architects*
Interior Consultants
Planners

100 South Fourth Street   Suite 700
St. Louis, Missouri 63102

90

NOVO

A graphic design trade school.

DESIGN FIRM:

Hegstrom Design, Auburn, California

ART DIRECTORS/ DESIGNERS:

Ken Hegstrom, Keoki Williams

ILLUSTRATOR:

Ken Hegstrom

Novo Design Center
19 North Second Street
San Jose, CA 95113
408.286-6686

Ken Hegstrom

NOVO

Novo Design Center *Registration Form*

NOVO

Last Name	First	Middle	
Address	Street		Apartment Number
City	State		Zip Code
( ) Daytime Phone		( ) Evening Phone	
Social Security Number	Date of Birth	Person to contact in case of emergency	Phone

Please give brief history of personal art and design education:

Name of School	Description of Class/Classes
Name of School	Description of Class/Classes
Name of School	Description of Class/Classes

Please give brief history of design-related work experience (if any):

Employer/Job Description
Employer/Job Description

Course Selection:
Because of the concentration required for each class, they must be taken consecutively– one per semester.

	Tuition:
❏ First Semester Introduction to Graphic Design:	$ 700.00
❏ Second Semester Design Applications:	700.00
❏ Third Semester Advanced Design Techniques:	700.00
❏ Fourth Semester The Business of Graphic Design:	700.00

$35. Portfolio Review Fee _____

Sub Total _____

–Discount: _____

Total: _____

Fill out application completely, including your signature, in order to register.

As a student of Novo Design Center, I hereby agree to abide by all policies and regulations of the school.

As a charter student at Novo Design Center, a discount of $25. may be taken for pre-enrollment in two semesters– $50. for three semesters– and $100. for all four semesters.

Make Check or Money Order payable to Novo Design Center.
Credit Cards Not Accepted.

Acceptance is based on a portfolio review by the faculty of Novo. If an applicant is not initially accepted, Novo will give a full and prompt refund of tuition paid, minus the portfolio review fee..

Signature of Applicant	Date

Send Registration Form and Tuition to:
Novo Design Center 19 North Second Street, Suite 202, San Jose, CA 95113

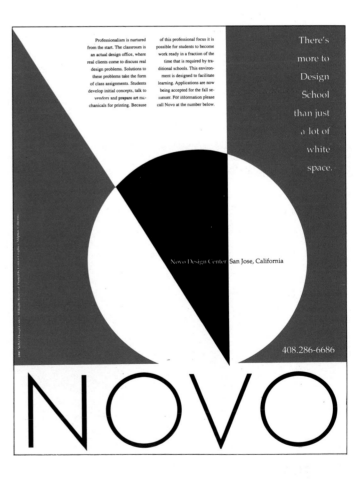

Professionalism is nurtured from the start. The classroom is an actual design office, where real clients come to discuss real design problems. Solutions to these problems take the form of class assignments. Students develop initial concepts, talk to vendors and prepare art mechanicals for printing. Because of this professional focus it is possible for students to become work ready in a fraction of the time that is required by traditional schools. This environment is designed to facilitate learning. Applications are now being accepted for the fall semester. For information please call Novo at the number below.

There's more to Design School than just a lot of white space.

Novo Design Center San Jose, California

408.286-6686

NOVO

School of Visual Arts

DESIGN FIRM:

Koppel & Scher, Inc.,

New York, New York

DESIGNER: Paula Scher

LA SPORTS

DESIGN FIRM:

Bright & Associates,

Venice, California

ART DIRECTOR:

Keith Bright

DESIGNER: Raymond Wood

Los Angeles Sports Council

California Melt

A gourmet sandwich

restaurant.

DESIGN FIRM:

Maureen Erbe Design,

Los Angeles, California

DESIGNER: Maureen Erbe

CALIFORNIA MELT

DESIGN FIRM:

Solutions By Design,

Fresno, California

DESIGNER: Charles Shields

ILLUSTRATOR:

Jane Bowden

California Fig Institute

3425 NORTH FIRST STREET
SUITE 109
FRESNO, CALIFORNIA 93726
(209) 224-5447
(209) 445-5626
FAX (209) 224-5449

A public-service campaign
sponsored by S.C.
Johnson's Deep Woods Off!
insect repellent and
American Forestry
Association.

DESIGN FIRM:

Mintz & Hoke, Avon,

Connecticut

DESIGNER: Dana Robinson

ILLUSTRATOR: Eric Spencer

SYSTEM ! K ®

System K (Computer Training)

DESIGN FIRM:

Fleury Design, Huntington

Station, New York

DESIGNER: Ellen Fleury

SYSTEM

SYSTEM ! K

!

K

SYSTEM ! K
Computer Training Division of Gloria K School

500 Northern Blvd., Great Neck, New York 11021
516 487-7217   718 423-4444

SYSTEM ! K

ABLE-2

Campaign targeting
handicapped clients of a
computer systems supplier.
DESIGNER:
Mignon Khargie, Baltimore,
Maryland
CLIENT:
Automated Business
Systems & Services

The Circles Program (Philanthropic Society)

DESIGN FIRM:
Cowell Design Group,
Burbank, California
ART DIRECTOR: Lee Cowell
DESIGNER: Kevin Weinman
CLIENT: United Way

THE   CIRCLES   PROGRAM

DESIGN FIRM:

Plain Vanilla Graphics,

Denver, Colorado

DESIGNER: Gary Christlieb

ILLUSTRATOR:

Shawn Berlute-Shea

CLIENT: Doug Burton,

Trout Consultant

Doug Burton (Fly Fishing Guide)

Photo: John Weathersby

EVANSTON

E·T·H·N·I·C

ARTS

FESTIVAL

DESIGN FIRM:

Art on the Loose, Chicago,

Illinois

DESIGNER/ILLUSTRATOR:

Vernon Lockhart

CLIENT:

Evanston Arts Council

Evanston Ethnic Arts Festival

98

Taylor/Christian Advertising

?.............!

IDEAS THAT WORK.

TAYLOR/CHRISTIAN ADVERTISING, INC.
8035 BROADWAY
SAN ANTONIO, TEXAS 78209
(512) 829-1700
FAX 829-1973

Symbols for women's and
men's bathrooms.
DESIGN FIRM:
D'Auria Design, Bayside,
New York
ART DIRECTOR/
DESIGNER: Karen D'Auria

DESIGN FIRM:

The Graphics Studio,

Los Angeles, California

DESIGNER:

Gerry Rosentswieg

Key Consulting Group

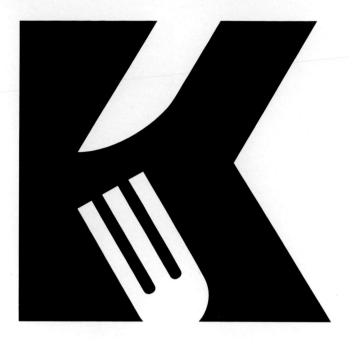

Gourmet kitchen architects

& consultants.

DESIGN FIRM:

Hegstrom Design, Auburn,

California

DESIGNER/ILLUSTRATOR:

Ken Hegstrom

Kelly Wayne Kitchens

A firm that designs and

writes health-related

materials.

DESIGN FIRM:

Steele Graphic Design,

Annandale, Virginia

ART DIRECTOR/

DESIGNER:

Carolyn C. Steele

HealthWrite Designs

HealthWrite Designs

HealthWrite Designs
4954 Sauquoit Lane
Annandale, VA 22003
CAROLYN C. STEELE   703/354-4193

HealthWrite Designs
5430 30th Street, N.W. • Washington, D.C. 20015

Catherine Avery: 5430 30th Street, N.W. • Washington, D.C. 20015 • 202/362-5390
Carolyn C. Steele: 4954 Sauquoit Lane • Annandale, VA 22003 • 703/354-4193

DESIGN FIRM:

T&A Design, New York,

New York

DESIGNER: Giulio Turturro

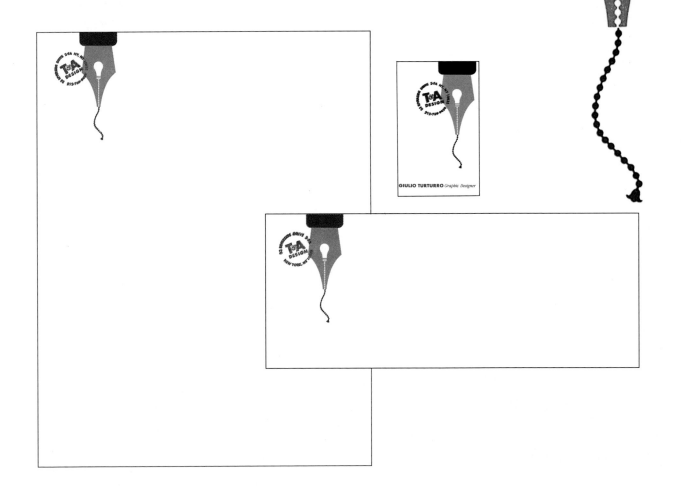

DESIGN FIRM:

Ingraham & Associates

Advertising, Durango,

Colorado

DESIGNER: Jane Ingraham

STIX (Chinese Restaurant Chain)

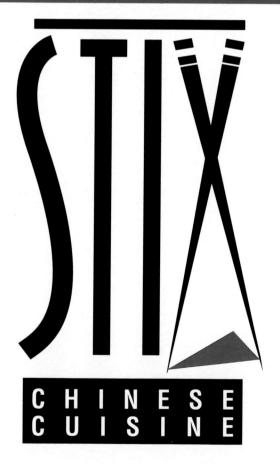

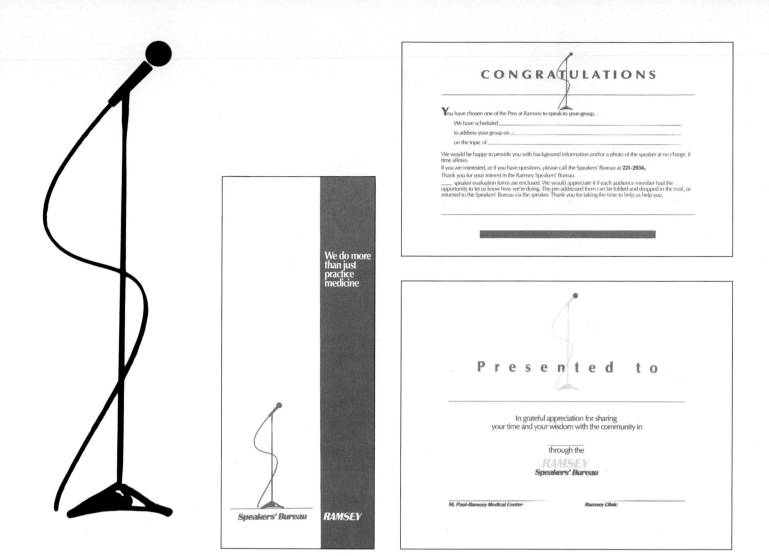

We do more than just practice medicine

Speakers' Bureau **RAMSEY**

CONGRATULATIONS

You have chosen one of the Pros at Ramsey to speak to your group.

We have scheduled _____

to address your group on : _____

on the topic of _____

We would be happy to provide you with background information and/or a photo of the speaker at no charge, if time allows.

If you are interested, or if you have questions, please call the Speakers' Bureau at **221-2934.**

Thank you for your interest in the Ramsey Speakers' Bureau.

_____ speaker evaluation forms are enclosed. We would appreciate it if each audience member had the opportunity to let us know how we're doing. The pre-addressed form can be folded and dropped in the mail, or returned to the Speakers' Bureau via the speaker. Thank you for taking the time to help us help you.

P r e s e n t e d   t o

_____

In grateful appreciation for sharing
your time and your wisdom with the community in

_____

through the

RAMSEY
Speakers' Bureau

_____   _____
St. Paul-Ramsey Medical Center   *Ramsey Clinic*

Ramsey Speakers' Bureau

Public service providing

health-care professionals to

speak to community

groups.

DESIGN FIRM:

Medical Media Services,

St. Paul, Minnesota

DESIGNER:

Timothy T. Trost

Speakers' Bureau

C O N F I R M A T I O N   F O R M

To: _____

This is to confirm that you have been scheduled to make a presentation as a member of the Ramsey Speakers' Bureau. The details are listed below. If you have any questions or are unable to make the presentation, please call Jane Schwanke, public relations, or the contact person.

Topic _____

Date of Speech _____

Name of Group _____

Size of Group _____ Age Range of Group _____

Address _____

_____

Time of Speech _____

Length of Speech _____

Question/Answer Period _____

Contact Person _____

Telephone _____

Notes _____

_____

Thank you for donating your time and sharing your expertise.

DESIGN FIRM:

Aufuldish & Warinner,

Larkspur, California

DESIGNER: Bob Aufuldish

Minneapolis College of Art & Design

DESIGN FIRM:

C.S. Anderson Design Co.,

Minneapolis, Minnesota

DESIGNERS: C.S. Anderson,

Dan Olson

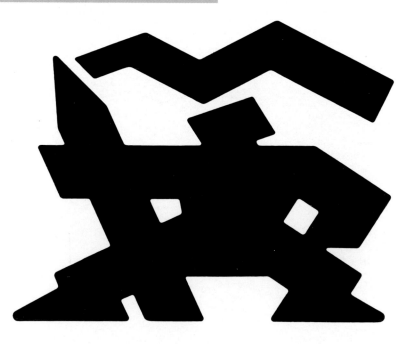

Northwest region skiing

competition.

DESIGN FIRM:

Werkhaus, Seattle,

Washington

DESIGNERS:

James Sundstad

CLIENT:

PNSA Freestyle Tour

DESIGN FIRM:

Jack Tom Design,

New York, New York

DESIGNER/ILLUSTRATOR:

Jack Tom

Jack Tom Design

DESIGN FIRM:

Celeski Studios, Seattle,

Washington

DESIGNER: Tim Celeski

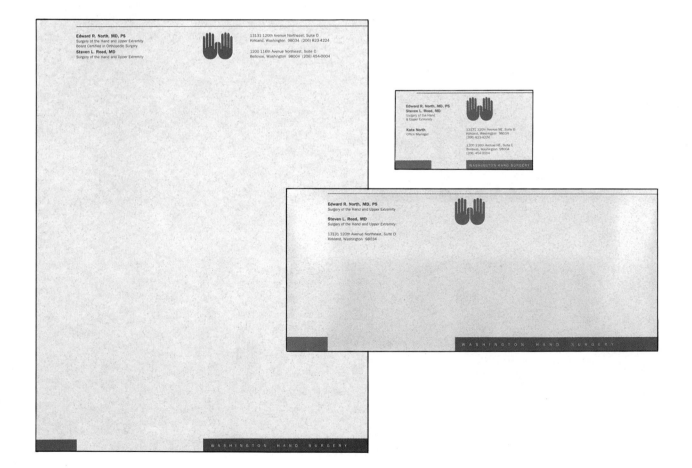

Edward R. North, MD, PS
Surgery of the Hand and Upper Extremity
Board Certified in Orthopedic Surgery
Steven L. Reed, MD
Surgery of the Hand and Upper Extremity

13131 120th Avenue Northeast, Suite D
Kirkland, Washington 98034 (206) 823-4224

1200 116th Avenue Northeast, Suite C
Bellevue, Washington 98004 (206) 454-0004

WASHINGTON HAND SURGERY

Edward R. North, MD, PS
Steven L. Reed, MD
Surgery of the Hand
& Upper Extremity

Kate North
Office Manager

13131 120th Avenue NE, Suite D
Kirkland, Washington 98034
(206) 823-4224

1200 116th Avenue NE, Suite C
Bellevue, Washington 98004
(206) 454-0004

WASHINGTON HAND SURGERY

Edward R. North, MD, PS
Surgery of the Hand and Upper Extremity

Steven L. Reed, MD
Surgery of the Hand and Upper Extremity

13131 120th Avenue Northeast, Suite D
Kirkland, Washington 98034

WASHINGTON HAND SURGERY

108

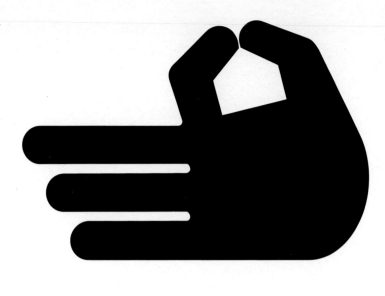

Mortgage Loans America

"Speedy Advance Approval

Service" program.

DESIGN FIRM:

Hegstrom Design, Auburn,

California

DESIGNER/ILLUSTRATOR:

Ken Hegstrom

Michael D. Nelson, D.D.S.

DESIGN FIRM:

Three Friends Design

Studio, Redding, California

DESIGNERS: Roy Maloney,

Gary FitzGerald

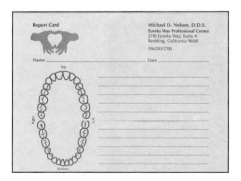

Annual awareness
campaign.
DESIGN FIRM:
National Technical Institute
for the Deaf, Rochester
Institute of Technology,
Rochester, New York
DESIGNER: L. Dean Woolever

Executive Development Inc.

DESIGN FIRM: Image Design,
Nashville, Tennessee
DESIGNER:
Linda Lerchenfeld

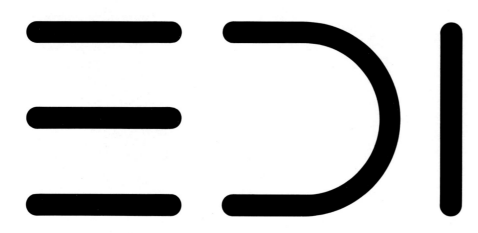

Executive Development Inc.

Asymetrix Corp. (Software)

DESIGN FIRM:

Hornall Anderson Design

Works, Seattle, Washington

ART DIRECTOR/

DESIGNER: Jack Anderson

DESIGNERS:

Heidi Hatlestad, Juliet Shen

DCA

Digital Communications Association (Software)

DESIGN FIRM:

Anspach Grossman

Portugal, New York,

New York

ART DIRECTOR:

Kenneth D. Love

DESIGNER: Jane Simonson

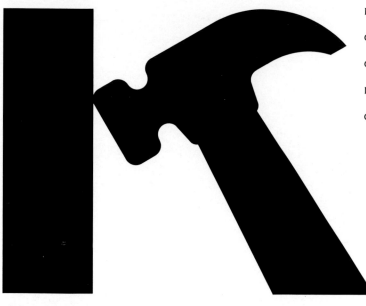

DESIGN FIRM:

Gil Shuler Graphic Design,

Charleston, South Carolina

DESIGNER/ILLUSTRATOR:

Gil Shuler

Stephen Koenig Construction

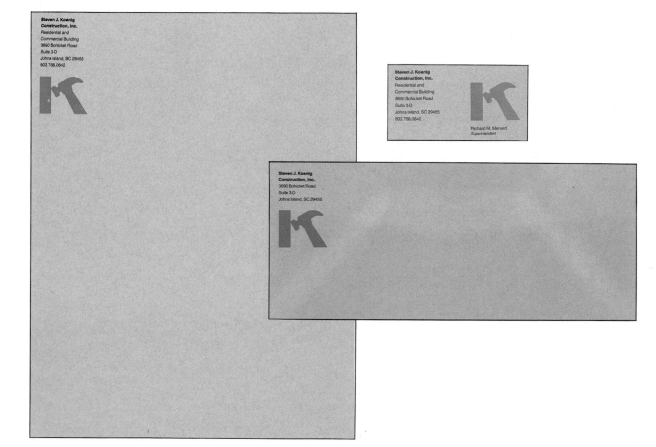

Steven J. Koenig
Construction, Inc.
Residential and
Commercial Building
3690 Bohicket Road
Suite 3-D
Johns Island, SC 29455
803.768.0642

Steven J. Koenig
Construction, Inc.
Residential and
Commercial Building
3690 Bohicket Road
Suite 3-D
Johns Island, SC 29455
803.768.0642

Richard M. Menard
Superintendent

Steven J. Koenig
Construction, Inc.
3690 Bohicket Road
Suite 3-D
Johns Island, SC 29455

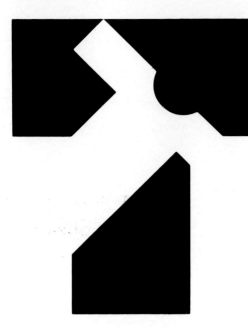

DESIGN FIRM:

Pictogram Studio,

Washington, DC

ART DIRECTOR/

DESIGNER: Hien Nguyen

DESIGNER:

Stephanie Hooten

Capital Tees (Imprinted T-Shirts & Sportswear)

CapitalTees

6925 Willow Street, NW
Washington, DC 20012
(202) 722-4721

CapitalTees

Joe Silberlicht

6925 Willow Street, NW
Washington, DC 20012
(202) 722-4721

*Quality imprinted
T-shirts and sportswear*

CapitalTees

6925 Willow Street, NW
Washington, DC 20012

Quality imprinted T-shirts and sportswear

Quality imprinted T-shirts and sportswear

Marie Weaver (Graduate Thesis)

DESIGN FIRM:

Weaver Design,

Birmingham, Alabama

DESIGNER: Marie Weaver

Wild Oats Productions (Greeting Cards)

DESIGN FIRM:

Murrie-White, Drummond,

Lienhart & Associates,

Chicago, Illinois

DESIGNER: Jim Lienhart

ILLUSTRATOR: Don Tate

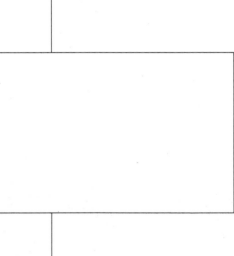

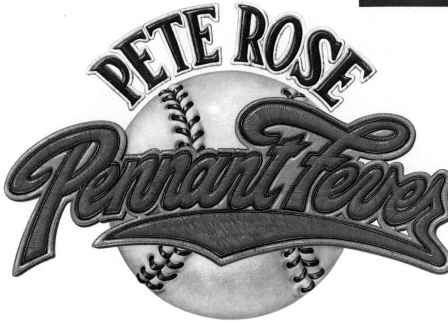

Pete Rose Pennant Fever (Computer Game)

DESIGN FIRM:

Mediagenic in-house design,

Menlo Park, California

DESIGNER: Bob Schonfisch

ILLUSTRATOR:

Michael Steirnagle

CLIENT: Gamestar

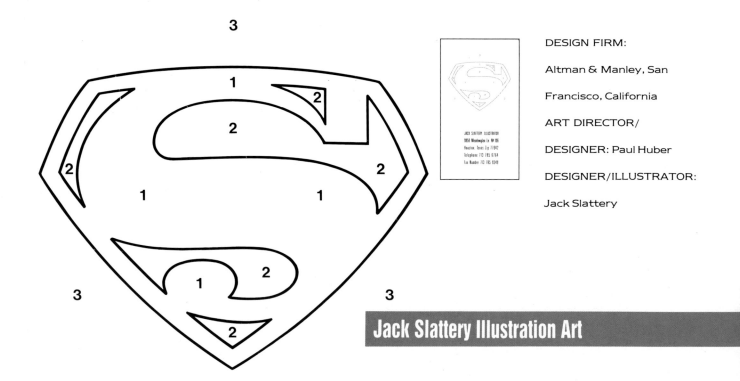

3

1

2

2

2

2

2

1

1

1

2

1

3

3

DESIGN FIRM:

Altman & Manley, San

Francisco, California

ART DIRECTOR/

DESIGNER: Paul Huber

DESIGNER/ILLUSTRATOR:

Jack Slattery

Jack Slattery Illustration Art

Commissioned by the Alliance Française, the French Government Tourist Office, and the French Chamber of Commerce to commemorate the 200th Anniversary of the storming of the Bastille.

DESIGN FIRM:
Zachow Design, Dallas, Texas

DESIGNER/ILLUSTRATOR:
Ed Zachow

CLIENTS:
The Beaird Agency, Inc., Kenneth H. Hughes, Inc.

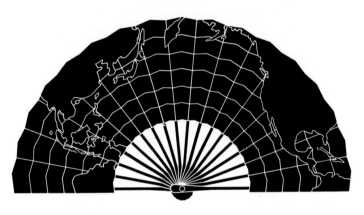

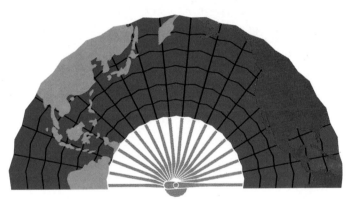

THE PACIFIC CENTURY THE PACIFIC CENTURY

A PBS television series on the historical conditions influencing present Pacific Rim countries.

DESIGN FIRM:
Ken Parkhurst & Associates, Los Angeles, California

ART DIRECTOR:
Ken Parkhurst

DESIGNER:
Denis Parkhurst

PROJECT MANAGER:
Kerry Neal

CLIENT: Jig Saw Productions

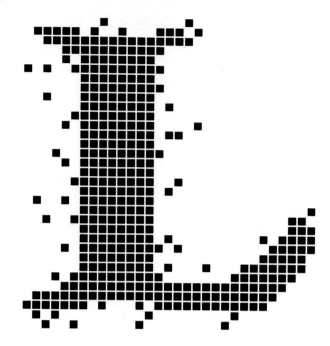

Letterforms (Typesetting & Output Consultants)

DESIGN FIRM:

Tom Carroll Design, Dracut,

Massachusetts

ART DIRECTORS:

Neil MacDonald, Gary

Fish/Designline

DESIGNER: Tom Carroll

Gullickson Illustration Design

DESIGNER: Vicki Gullickson,

Denver, Colorado

119

MOTHER LODE

MINITHON

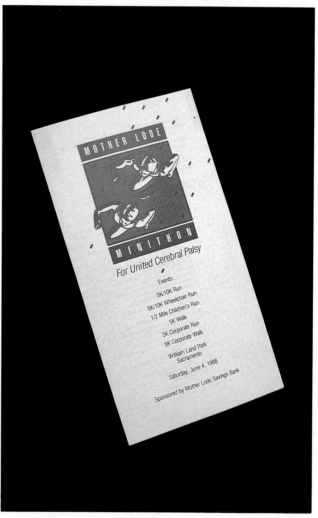

Benefit race for United

Cerebral Palsy sponsored   & Siegel, Sacramento,

by Mother Lode Savings   California

Bank.   ART DIRECTOR/

DESIGN FIRM: DESIGNER/ILLUSTRATOR:

Runyon Saltzman Weagraff   Steve Godfrey

Mother Lode Minithon

"Let the games begin."

Summer promotion using

the Olympics as a theme.

DESIGN FIRM: Tharp Did It,

Los Gatos, California

DESIGNER: Rick Tharp

Carry Nation's (Bar)

DESIGN FIRM:

The Idea Department,

St. Louis, Missouri

ART DIRECTOR:

Maris Cirulis

DESIGNER:

Jennifer Anderson

The Idea Department

A firm that manufactures and services computer hardware.
DESIGN FIRM:
A&K Advertising, Arlington, Texas
ART DIRECTOR/
DESIGNER: Dennis Gore

A group of eight different, but related, businesses offering clients a total marketing package.
DESIGN FIRM:
Galarneau & Sinn, Palo Alto, California
DESIGNER/ILLUSTRATOR:
Mark Galarneau

Octagon

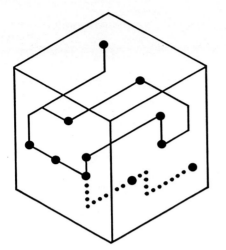

DESKTALK

A firm that integrates
computer systems and
networks and develops
programs.

DESIGN FIRM:
Louey/Rubino Design
Group, Santa Monica,
California

ART DIRECTOR:
Regina Rubino

DESIGNER: Robert Louey

A national distributor of paper and business supplies.

DESIGN FIRM:
Graphic Design Continuum, Dayton, Ohio

DESIGNER:
Dwayne Swormstedt

Zellerbach

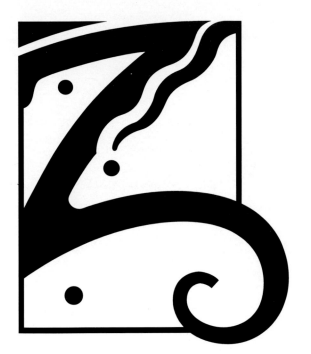

Sacramento Zoo

DESIGN FIRM:

Tackett-Barbaria Design,

Sacramento, California

DESIGNERS:

Steve Barbaria (logo),

Steve Ball (vehicle graphic),

Bob Dahlquist (poster)

Piece of Cake (Catering)

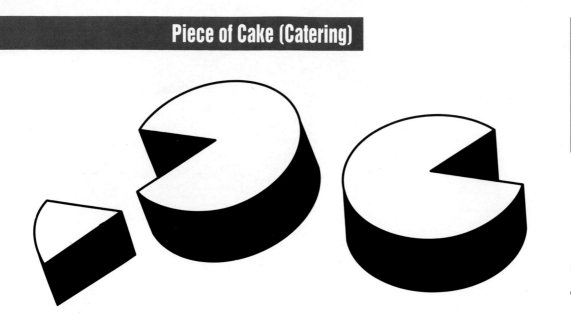

DESIGN FIRM:

Klingemann Illustration &

Design, Lewisville, Texas

DESIGNER/ILLUSTRATOR:

Gary Klingemann

Fresh Eats (Salad Bar Restaurant)

DESIGN FIRM: Tharp Did It,

Los Gatos, California

ART DIRECTOR/

DESIGNER: Rick Tharp

DESIGNER: Kim Tomlinson

DESIGN FIRM:

Stephen Bodkin Design,

New York, New York

DESIGNER: Stephen Bodkin

Say Cheese Shops

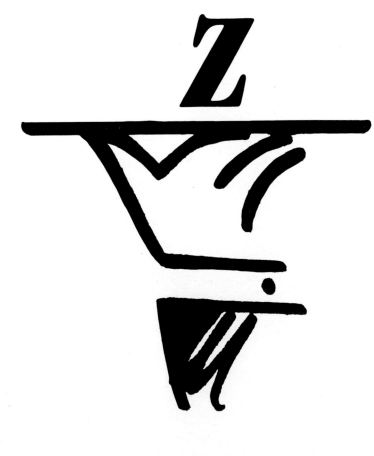

DESIGN FIRM:

Bianco Marchilonis Design,

Needham, Massachusetts

DESIGNER/ILLUSTRATOR:

Peter Bianco

Zipper Catering Service

ONE MARKET
PLAZA

DESIGN FIRM:

William Reuter Design,

San Francisco, California

DESIGNER: William Reuter

Richard J. Leider
Senior Sales Consultant

Coldwell Banker Commercial
Real Estate Services

Exclusive Leasing Agent
Embarcadero Center West
275 Battery Street, Suite 1300
San Francisco, California 94111-3305

415.772.0225   Fax 415.772.0459

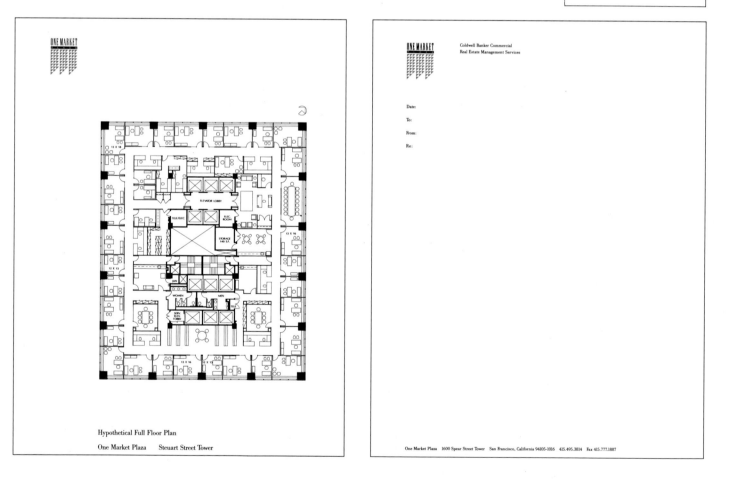

Hypothetical Full Floor Plan

One Market Plaza   Steuart Street Tower

Coldwell Banker Commercial
Real Estate Management Services

Date:

To:

From:

Re:

One Market Plaza   1600 Spear Street Tower   San Francisco, California 94105-1016   415.495.3814   Fax 415.777.1887

DESIGN FIRM:

West Associates Advertising

& Design, Leawood, Kansas

DESIGNERS:

Stan Chrzanowski, Jack

Swearengin

Langley Group (Travel Agency)

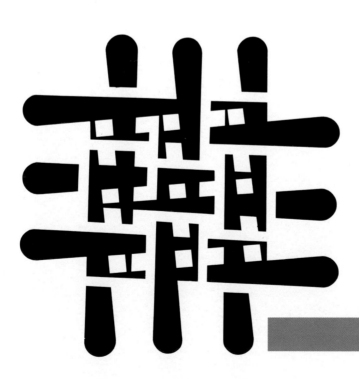

A weaving and lacemaking

studio.

DESIGN FIRM:

Slanting Rain Graphic

Design, Logan, Utah

DESIGNER: R.P. Bissland

Interlace Fiber Arts

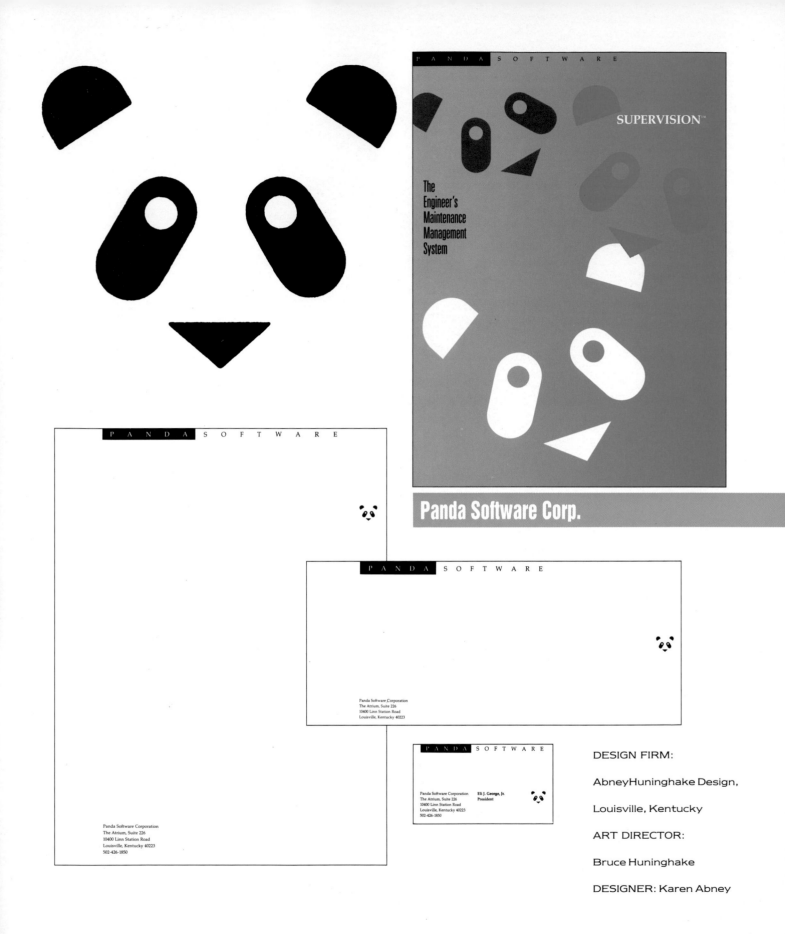

PANDA SOFTWARE

SUPERVISION™

The
Engineer's
Maintenance
Management
System

Panda Software Corp.

PANDA SOFTWARE

Panda Software Corporation
The Atrium, Suite 226
10400 Linn Station Road
Louisville, Kentucky 40223
502-426-1850

PANDA SOFTWARE

Panda Software Corporation
The Atrium, Suite 226
10400 Linn Station Road
Louisville, Kentucky 40223

PANDA SOFTWARE

Panda Software Corporation   Eli J. George, Jr.
The Atrium, Suite 226   President
10400 Linn Station Road
Louisville, Kentucky 40223
502-426-1850

DESIGN FIRM:

AbneyHuninghake Design,

Louisville, Kentucky

ART DIRECTOR:

Bruce Huninghake

DESIGNER: Karen Abney

DESIGN FIRM:

Linda Unger Design, Dallas,

Texas

DESIGNER:

Linda Eissler Unger

A landscape design and
installation office.
DESIGN FIRM:
Kris Morgan Design,
Seattle, Washington
DESIGNER: Kris Morgan

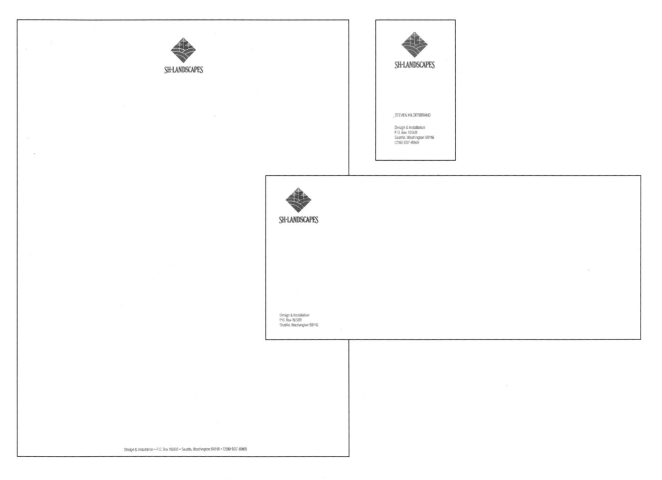

DESIGN FIRM:

Pictogram Studio,

Washington, DC

DESIGNER:

Stephanie Hooton

ILLUSTRATOR: Hien Nguyen

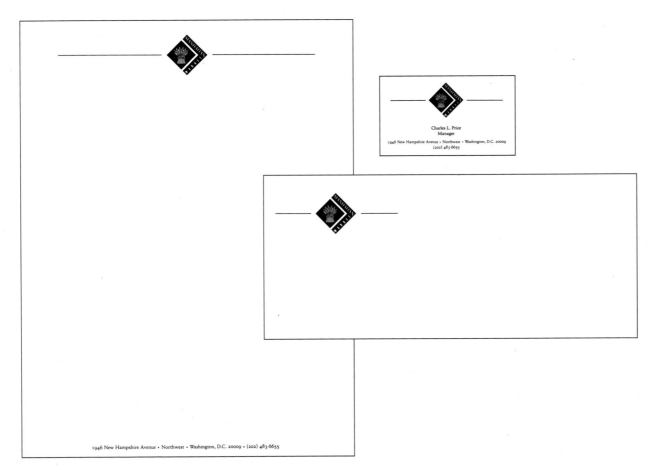

John H. Harland Co.

Promotion for a check printer's new facility in Wilkes Barre, Pennsylvania.
DESIGN FIRM:
Internal Design Group of John H. Harland Co., Decatur, Georgia
ART DIRECTOR:
Mary Dubois
DESIGNER: Joe Alcober

DESIGN FIRM:

The Weller Institute for the

Cure of Design, Park City,

Utah

DESIGNER: Don Weller

Park City Historical Society & Museum

DESIGN FIRM:

Mañana Design, Burlington,

Vermont

Designer: Anthony Sini

Vermont Bagel Works

An environmental radio

program.

DESIGN FIRM:

Louise Fili Ltd., New York,

New York

DESIGNER: Louise Fili

ILLUSTRATOR:

Anthony Russo

Linda Hayes, Associate Producer
(212) 473-2918

RD 1, Box 108 · Croton Heights Rd. · Yorktown Heights, N.Y. 10598 · (914) 962-1751 · FAX: 962-1752 · Jim Metzner, Executive Producer

108 Croton Heights Rd. · Yorktown Heights, N.Y. 10598

DESIGN FIRM:

Golem Graphix, Arlington,

Virginia

DESIGNER: Gregory Golem

INSPIRATION: Betsey Golem

Samaritan Health Services

DESIGN FIRM:

SBG Partners,

San Francisco, California

ART DIRECTORS:

Nicolas Sidjakov, Jerry

Berman

DESIGNER: Jackie Foshaug

ILLUSTRATOR:

Rebecca Archey

PROGRAM DIRECTOR:

Michael Purvis

ACCOUNT DIRECTOR:

Liz Albrecht

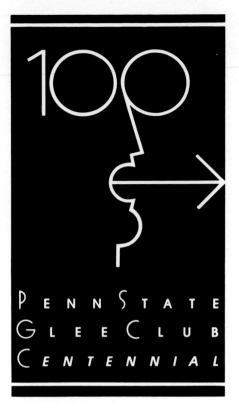

DESIGN FIRM:

Sommese Design, State

College, Pensylvania

ART DIRECTOR/

DESIGNER:

Lanny Sommese

DESIGNER:

Kristin Sommese

Penn State Glee Club (100th Anniversary)

DESIGN FIRM:

Graham Spencer

Advertising/Design,

Rockford, Illinois

DESIGNERS: Jay Graham,

Scott Spencer

No Boring Clothes (Retail)

Richardson Restoration & Machine Werks

A firm specializing in the rebuilding and repair of Mercedes Benz 300SL automobiles with an emphasis on mechanical restoration.

DESIGN FIRM:

Richardson or Richardson, Phoenix, Arizona

ART DIRECTOR:

Forrest Richardson

DESIGNER: Jim Bolek

RICHARDS●N RESTORA♦ION & MACH█NE WERKS

RICHARDS●N RESTORA♦ION & MACH█NE WERKS

Scottsdale Airpark
7350 East Acoma Drive
Scottsdale, Arizona 85260
602.948.4372

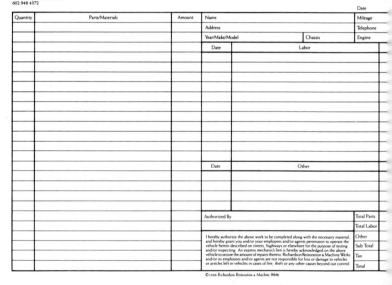

RICHARDS●N RESTORA♦ION & MACH█NE WERKS

Scottsdale Airpark
7350 East Acoma Drive
Scottsdale, Arizona 85260
602.948.4372

Quantity	Parts/Materials	Amount	Name		Date
					Mileage
			Address		Telephone
			Year/Make/Model	Chassis	Engine
			Date	Labor	
			Date	Other	
			Authorized By		Total Parts
					Total Labor
			I hereby authorize the above work to be completed along with the necessary material, and hereby grant you and/or your employees and/or agents permission to operate the vehicle herein described on streets, highways or elsewhere for the purpose of testing and/or inspecting. An express mechanic's lien is hereby acknowledged on the above vehicle to secure the amount of repairs thereto. Richardson Restoration & Machine Werks and/or its employees and/or agents are not responsible for loss or damage to vehicles or articles left in vehicles in cases of fire, theft or any other causes beyond our control.		Other
					Sub Total
					Tax
					Total

©1988 Richardson Restoration & Machine Werks

RICHARDS●N

Bill Richardson

Scottsdale Airpark
7350 East Acoma Drive
Scottsdale, Arizona 85260
602.948.4372

E(((ENTRI(S

DESIGN FIRM:

Anton Kimball Design,

Portland, Oregon

DESIGNER/ILLUSTRATOR:

Anton Kimball

FACE TO FACE

It's a beauty fair at Dayton's.

Dayton Hudson (Department Store Cosmetics Promotion)

DESIGN FIRM:

Dayton Hudson

Department Store Co.,

Minneapolis, Minnesota

DESIGNER: Cheryl Watson

COPYWRITER:

Lisa Christensen

Bentley Mills

Logo series designed for a line of sportswear and gift items promoting a carpet manufacturer to its clients.

DESIGN FIRM:

Maureen Erbe Design,

Los Angeles, California

ART DIRECTOR:

Maureen Erbe

DESIGNERS:

Maureen Erbe, Holly

Caporale

DESIGN FIRM:

Kiku Obata & Co., St. Louis, Missouri

ART DIRECTOR:

Kiku Obata

DESIGNER/ILLUSTRATOR:

Ed Mantels-Seeker

CLIENT: Love Management

A benefit dance and auction

for the American Red Cross.

DESIGN FIRM:

Glenn Martinez &

Associates, Santa Rosa,

California

DESIGNER: Glenn Martinez

Shoes With Wings

S H O E S

W I T H !

W I N G S

A collaborative formed to provide personal, professional, and promotional support for 12 artist-mothers.

DESIGN FIRM:

Colvin/Williams,

Watertown, Massachusetts

ART DIRECTOR:

Susan Williams

ILLUSTRATOR:

Toby Williams

Art Moms

An independent video

production company.

DESIGN FIRM:

Ron Kellum Design,

New York, New York

DESIGNER/ILLUSTRATOR:

Ron Kellum

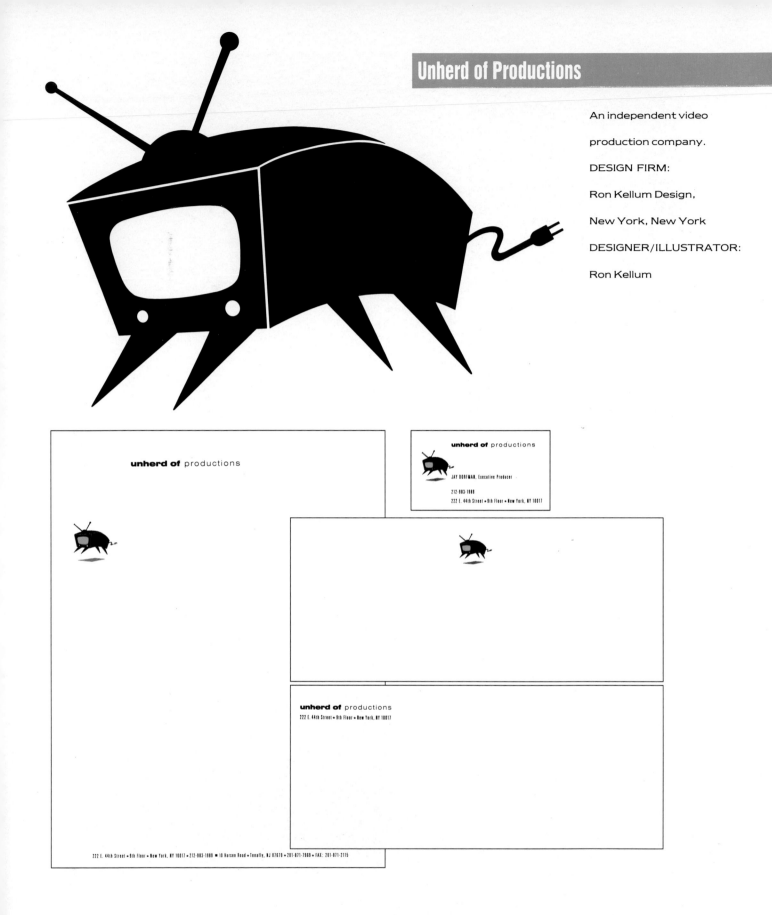

unherd of productions

unherd of productions

JAY DORFMAN, Executive Producer

212-983-1988

222 E. 44th Street • 9th Floor • New York, NY 10017

unherd of productions

222 E. 44th Street • 9th Floor • New York, NY 10017

222 E. 44th Street • 9th Floor • New York, NY 10017 • 212-983-1988 • 10 Hersen Road • Tenafly, NJ 07670 • 201-871-7969 • FAX: 201-871-2115

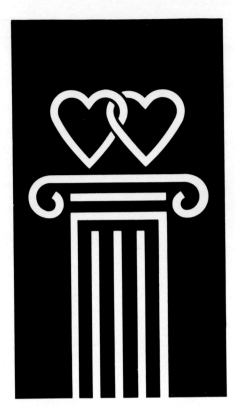

DESIGN FIRM:

Jim Nuttle Design, Silver

Spring, Maryland

DESIGNER: Jim Nuttle

Walter and Ruth Fahrig
request the honour of your presence
at the marriage of their daughter
Lenore
to
William Kensett Nuttle
on Saturday, the twenty-seventh of May
nineteen hundred and eighty-nine
at half past four in the afternoon
Saint Bartholomew's Anglican Church
125 MacKay Street, Ottawa

Reception dinner to follow at
the home of Walter and Ruth Fahrig

The favour of a reply is requested
76 Ryeburn Drive
Gloucester, Ontario
Canada K1G 3N3

International Resource Center

International textile trade

showrooms.

DESIGN FIRM:

Edward Walter Design,

New York, New York

DESIGNER/ILLUSTRATOR:

Edward Walter

A distributor of R-rated
videos that have been
edited for viewing by all age
groups.
DESIGNER: Art Lofgreen,
Phoenix, Arizona

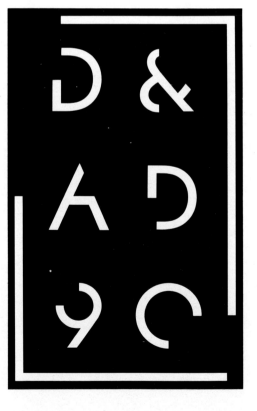

DESIGN FIRM: Pentagram,

New York, New York

DESIGNER: Woody Pirtle

D&AD (Designers & Art Directors Club, UK)

DESIGN FIRM:

Virginia Woodhead Design,

Alexandria, Virginia

ART DIRECTOR:

Nancy Gleeson

DESIGNER:

Virginia Woodhead

Alexandria High School Crew Program

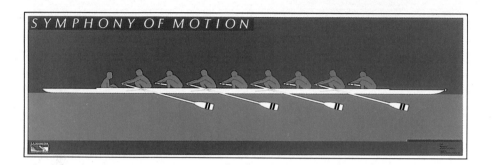

SYMPHONY OF MOTION

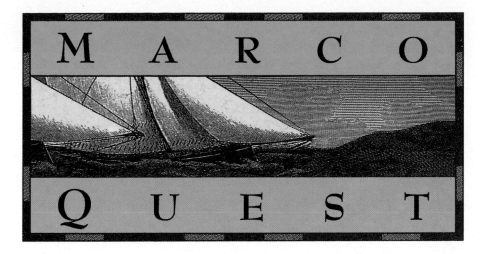

Sales-incentive travel

program.

DESIGN FIRM:

Mires Design, Inc., San

Diego, California

DESIGNER/ILLUSTRATOR:

Scott Mires

The Masters Group

Begin today with a healthy breakfast in the hotel. Please sign the check with your name, room number and "Miller Brewing Company." ••• 10:00 A.M. Competitive spirit runs high this morning as teams head for the beach and the Miller Lite Olympic Games! ••• You may use your cash allowance for lunch again today. ••• 7:00 P.M. Miller Lite "Marco Quest" winners enjoy the best food and hospitality in the South . . . with a "low country" shrimp and lobster bake! ••• After dinner, the Miller Lite Hospitality Suite will be open for your pleasure.

DAY THREE
Daytime Dress: Casual sportswear.
Evening Dress: Casual; jeans, shorts and
sweater.

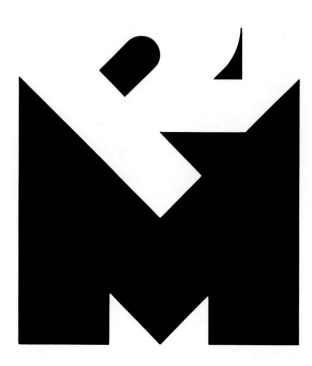

Rick Mariani Photography

DESIGN FIRM:

Jack Tom Design,

New York, New York

DESIGNER/ILLUSTRATOR:

Jack Tom

Peacock Construction

DESIGN FIRM:

Grand Pré & Whaley, Ltd.,

St. Paul, Minnesota

DESIGNER: Kevin Whaley

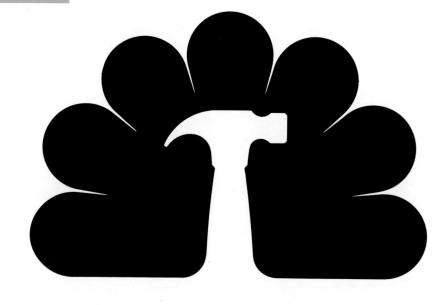

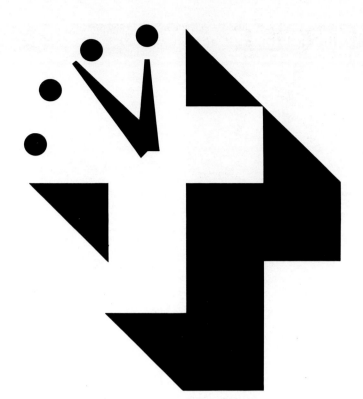

Program promoting the
ordaining of female clergy in
the Seventh-Day Adventist
Church.
DESIGN FIRM:
Dever Designs, Laurel,
Maryland
DESIGNER: Jeffrey L. Dever

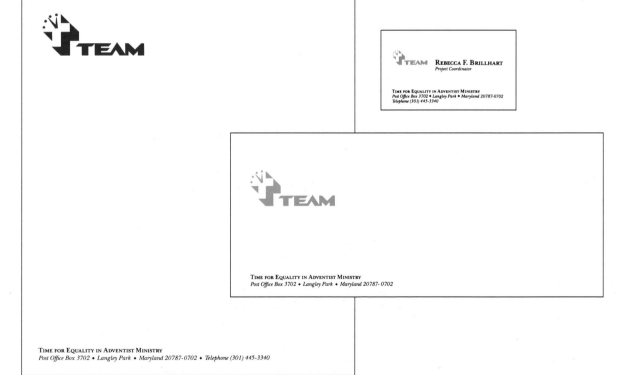

PRIMADONNA

DESIGN FIRM:

PrimaDonna, Detroit, Michigan

DESIGNER: Donna McGuire

COPYWRITER: Bill Cutter

PrimaDonna

PRIMADONNA

300-A Globe Building, 407 East Fort Street, Detroit, MI 48226

300-A Globe Building, 407 East Fort Street
DONNA McGUIRE ☏ 313/964/5610
Detroit, MI 48226 FAX (313) 964•3953

PRIMADONNA

PRIMADONNA

300-A Globe Building

407 East Fort Street

Detroit, Michigan 48226

(313) 964-5610

FAX (313) 964-3953

PRIMADONNA

300-A Globe Building

407 East Fort Street

Detroit, Michigan 48226

(313) 964-5610

FAX (313) 964-3953

ESTIMATE

Date

Job #

Client

Product/Title

Description

FEES

Art Direction/Design

Copywriting/Editing

Project Coordination

Printing Supervision

Assistant

EXPENSES

Comprehensive Mock-Up Materials

Photography

Illustration

Special Artwork

Retouching

Special Photostat Processes

Duplicate Prints/Color Prints

Type Test

Typography

Camera Ready Keyline

Photostats

White Prints/Negative

Art Supplies

Xerox/Fax

Couriers

Shipping/Insurance

Printing

SUBTOTAL FEES

SUBTOTAL EXPENSES

TOTAL

Line of tennis clothing
endorsed by tennis
champion Michael Chang
for Reebok.
DESIGN FIRM:
Victoria Miller Design,
Los Angeles, California
DESIGNER: Victoria Miller

A group that organizes
volunteer construction
projects around the world.
DESIGN FIRM: Boomerang,
Berrien Springs, Michigan
DESIGNER/ILLUSTRATOR:
Sheri Seibold

Maranatha Volunteers International

153

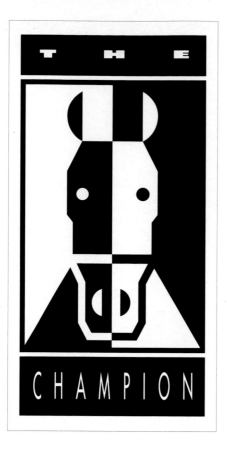

DESIGN FIRM:

The Design Group, JRSK,

Dallas, Texas

DESIGNER/ILLUSTRATOR:

Paul Black

COPYWRITER: Jim Sykora

CLIENT: Zoecon Corp.

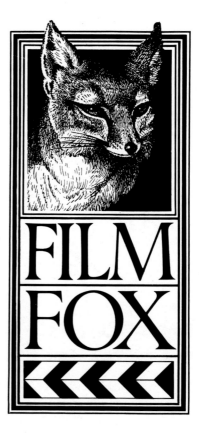

An independent

documentary film company

specializing in

environmental and social

projects.

DESIGN FIRM:

Ashby Design, Annapolis,

Maryland

DESIGNER: Neal M. Ashby

Film Fox

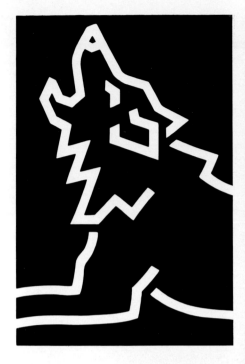

Thurston Wolfe Winery

DESIGN FIRM:

Jennifer Kennard Design,

Seattle, Washington

DESIGNER:

Jennifer Kennard

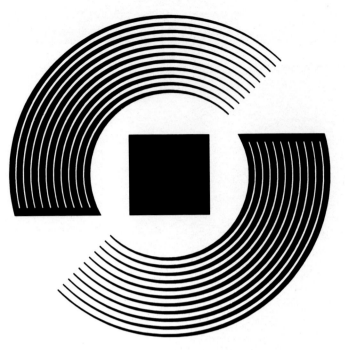

A manufacturer of

computerized

telecommunications

equipment.

DESIGN FIRM:

Knape&Knape, Dallas,

Texas

ART DIRECTOR:

Willie Baronet

DESIGNER/ILLUSTRATOR:

Michael Connors

Strategic Telecom

Al "Uncle Al" Budris
Proprietor

10033 Mann Drive
Cupertino, CA 95014
408.255.2925

DESIGN FIRM:

Hegstrom Design, Auburn,

California

DESIGNER: Ken Hegstrom

DESIGNER/ILLUSTRATOR:

John Stoneham/Stoneham

Design

CycleCraft (Bicycle Retailer)

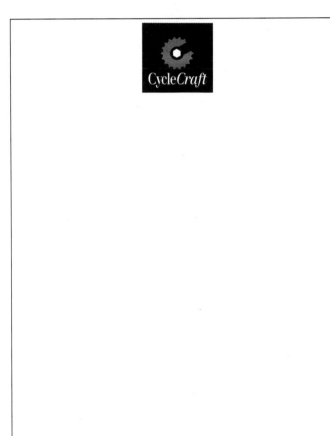

10033 Mann Drive, Cupertino, California 95014 408.255.2925

DESIGN FIRM:

Pannuzzo-Larimore, Inc.,

Albuquerque, New Mexico

ART DIRECTORS: Ron

Pannuzzo, J.C. Larimore,

Mark Chamberlain

DESIGNER: Ron Pannuzo

ILLUSTRATOR:

Mark Chamberlain

CLIENT: Doubletree Hotel

DESIGN FIRM:

Northeast Design Group,

Providence, Rhode Island

DESIGNERS: David Mealey,

Allen Wong

Providence Classical Concerts

PROVIDENCE
CLASSICAL
CONCERTS

LIGHT VERSE

Mary Ann Barton

203 Loudon Road #4-12
Concord, NH 03301
(603) 224-8963

*original verse and poetic prose
for special occasions*

DESIGNER/ILLUSTRATOR:

Beth Krommes, Rindge,

New Hampshire

TOLEDOFEST

A CELEBRATION OF THE ARTS

Toledofest (Outdoor Riverfront Festival)

DESIGN FIRM:

Communicā, Inc., Toledo,

Ohio

DESIGNER/ILLUSTRATOR:

Jeff Kimble

CLIENT: Arts Commission

of Greater Toledo

159

DESIGN FIRM: Pentagram,

New York, New York

ART DIRECTOR/

DESIGNER: Woody Pirtle

DESIGNER: Jennifer Long

Crossroads Film

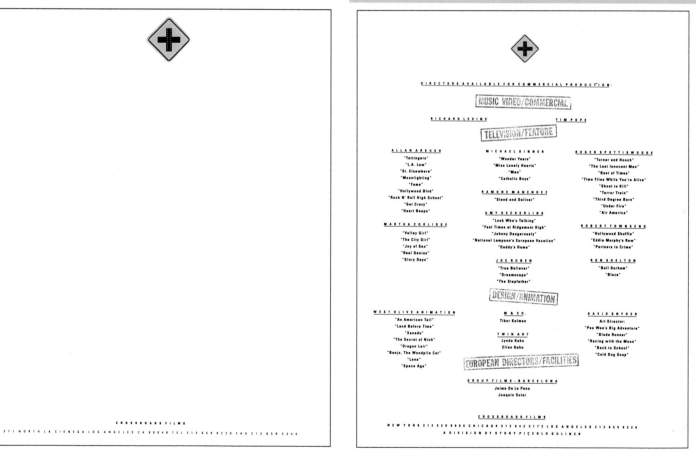

CROSSROADS FILMS
371 NORTH LA CIENEGA LOS ANGELES CA 90048 TEL 213 659 8220 FAX 213 659 2345

DIRECTORS AVAILABLE FOR COMMERCIAL PRODUCTION:

MUSIC VIDEO/COMMERCIAL

RICHARD LEVINE   TIM POPE

TELEVISION/FEATURE

ALLAN ARKUSH   MICHAEL DINNER   ROGER SPOTTISWOODE
"Tattingers"   "Wonder Years"   "Turner and Hooch"
"L.A. Law"   "Miss Lonely Hearts"   "The Last Innocent Man"
"St. Elsewhere"   "Men"   "Best of Times"
"Moonlighting"   "Catholic Boys"   "Time Flies While You're Alive"
"Fame"   "Shoot to Kill"
"Hollywood Blvd"   RAMONE MANENDEZ   "Terror Train"
"Rock N' Roll High School"   "Stand and Deliver"   "Third Degree Burn"
"Get Crazy"   "Under Fire"
"Heart Beeps"   AMY HECKERLING   "Air America"
                "Look Who's Talking"
MARTHA COOLIDGE   "Fast Times at Ridgemont High"   ROBERT TOWNSEND
"Valley Girl"   "Johnny Dangerously"   "Hollywood Shuffle"
"The City Girl"   "National Lampoon's European Vacation" "Eddie Murphy's Raw"
"Joy of Sex"   "Daddy's Home"   "Partners in Crime"
"Real Genius"
"Glory Days"   JOE RUBEN   RON SHELTON
                "True Believer"   "Bull Durham"
                "Dreamscape"   "Blaze"
                "The Stepfather"

DESIGN/ANIMATION

WEST OLIVE ANIMATION   M & CO.   DAVID SNYDER
"An American Tail"   Tibor Kalman   Art Director:
"Land Before Time"   "Pee Wee's Big Adventure"
"Xanadu"   TWIN ART   "Blade Runner"
"The Secret of Nimh"   Lynda Kahn   "Racing with the Moon"
"Dragon Lair"   Ellen Kahn   "Back to School"
"Banjo, The Woodpile Cat"   "Cold Dog Soup"
"Lena"
"Space Age"

EUROPEAN DIRECTORS/FACILITIES

GROUP FILMS - BARCELONA
Jaime De La Pena
Joaquin Soler

CROSSROADS FILMS
NEW YORK 212 529 9990 CHICAGO 212 642 3173 LOS ANGELES 213 659 8220
A DIVISION OF STORY PICCOLO GULINER

A mail-order company

specializing in photography

books.

DESIGN FIRM:

Toto Images, New York,

New York

ART DIRECTOR/

DESIGNER: Andy Lun

DESIGNER: Jeffrey Huang

Literature on Photography

NONNI'S

DESIGN FIRM:

Bruce Yelaska Design,

San Francisco, California

DESIGNER: Bruce Yelaska

Nonni's Biscotti (Bakery)

NONNI'S

2800 20TH STREET
SAN FRANCISCO, CA 94110
PHONE 415-648-3488
FAX 415-648-2480

STEVE SIRIANNI

NONNI'S

120 NANTUCKET COVE
SAN RAFAEL, CA 94001
415-457-1483

NONNI'S

129 NANTUCKET COVE
SAN RAFAEL, CA 94901

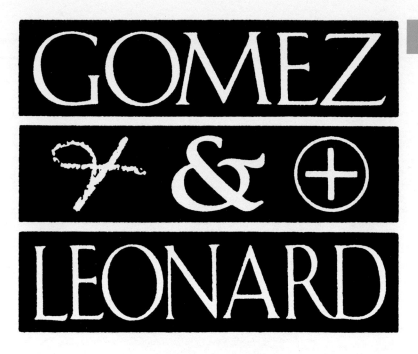

DESIGN FIRM:

Newman Design Associates

Inc., Guilford, Connecticut

DESIGNER: Bob Newman

Gomez & Leonard Public Relations
770 Towner Swamp Road
Guilford, Connecticut 06437
203 481 6717

Catherine G. Leonard

Gomez & Leonard Public Relations
770 Towner Swamp Road
Guilford, Connecticut 06437
203 481 6717

Gomez & Leonard Public Relations
770 Towner Swamp Road
Guilford, Connecticut 06437

Solo Editions

An advertising agency for
photographers, illustrators,
and artists representatives.

DESIGN FIRM:

The Pushpin Group,

New York, New York

ART DIRECTOR:

Seymour Chwast

DESIGNER/ILLUSTRATOR:

Greg Simpson

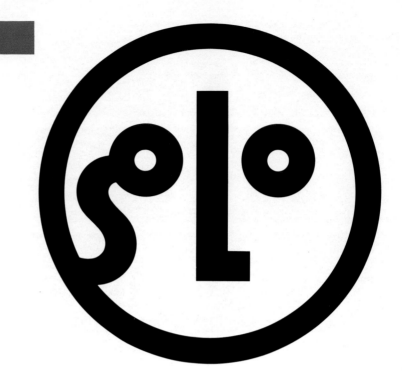

Homesmiths Home Maintenance

DESIGN FIRM:

Laurie R. Wicker Graphic

Design, Brooklyn,

New York

DESIGNER/ILLUSTRATOR:

Laurie R. Wicker

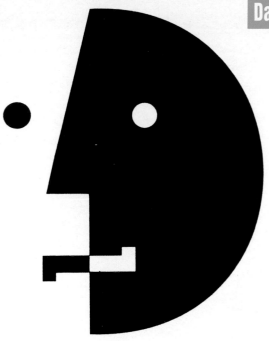

DESIGN FIRM:

Peterson & Company,

Dallas, Texas

DESIGNER: Scott Ray

DESIGN FIRM:

Red Top Design, Laguna

Beach, California

DESIGNER:

Michelle Svoboda

CLIENT:

Bobbie Kerns & Associates

BK&A Real-Estate Sales Seminars

Acadiana Truck Rental

DESIGN FIRM:

The Graham Group,

Lafayette, Louisiana

ART DIRECTOR/

DESIGNER/ILLUSTRATOR:

Tony Liu

Ferro+Ferro

DESIGN FIRM:

Ferro+Ferro Graphic

Communications, Arlington,

Virginia

ART DIRECTOR: Sam Ferro

DESIGNER: Dorothy Ferro

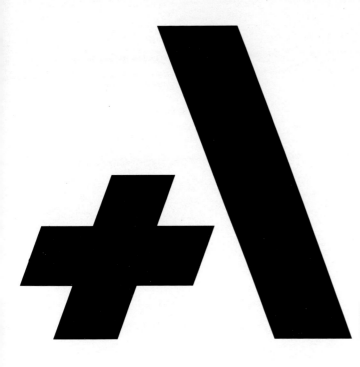

Developer, manufacturer,
and marketer of
sophisticated medical
equipment.
DESIGNER:
Ann Clementino,
Manchester, Connecticut

Advanced Pulmonary Technologies

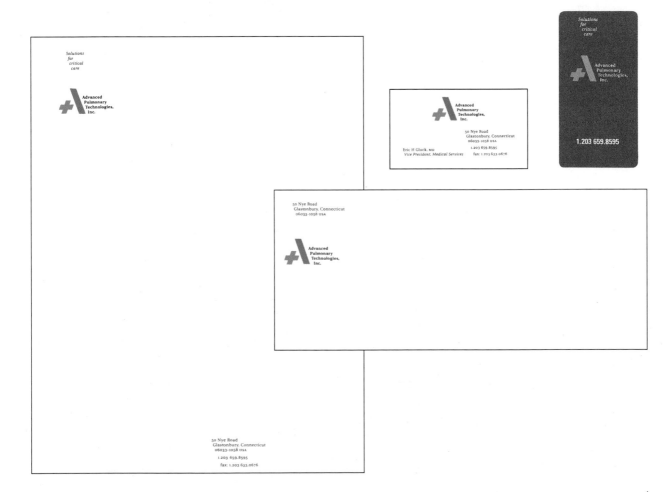

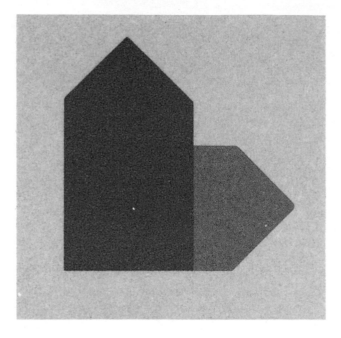

A family-owned architectural design, construction, and development company.
DESIGN FIRM: Puccinelli Design, Santa Barbara, California
DESIGNER: Keith Puccinelli

Lineage Homes

A firm providing
architectural, interior, and
graphic design services.
DESIGNER: Art Lofgreen,
Phoenix ,Arizona
ILLUSTRATOR:
Curtis Parker

Design Troupe

401 SOUTH MILL AVENUE, SUITE 201
TEMPE, ARIZONA 85281
602-894-4635, FAX 894-4647

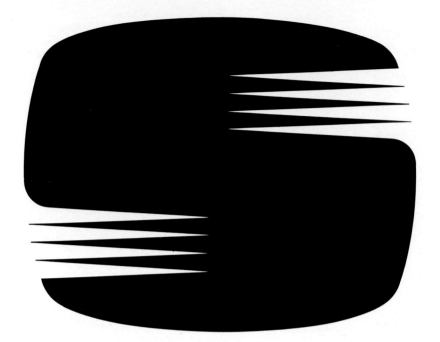

A video production

company.

DESIGN FIRM:

Bruce E. Morgan Graphic

Design, Washington, DC

ART DIRECTOR/

DESIGNER:

Bruce E. Morgan

Scherer & Sutherland Productions

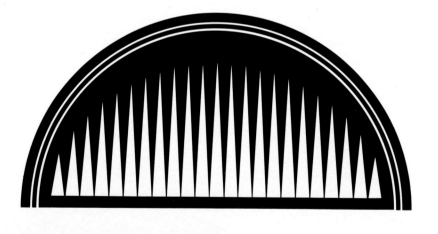

DESIGN FIRM:

Dan Frazier Design,

Redwood City, California

DESIGNER: Dan Frazier

Oakland Ensemble Theatre

DESIGN FIRM:

Nordstrom Advertising,

Seattle, Washington

ART DIRECTOR:

Cheryl Zahniser

DESIGNER: Judy Dolim

Nordstrom's Hoop Clothing Line

Created for Texas

Instruments to

commemorate Earth Day.

DESIGN FIRM: Tom Hair

Marketing Design, Dallas,

Texas

ART DIRECTOR: Tom Hair

ART DIRECTOR/

DESIGNER: Brian Collins

Earth Day

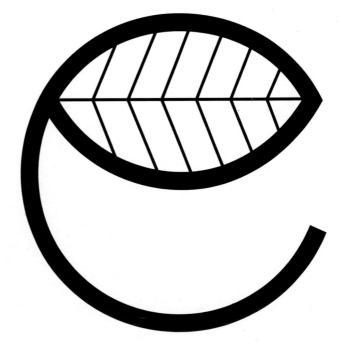

171

A non-profit organization

dedicated to river

conservation.

DESIGN FIRM:

William Homan Design,

Minnetonka, Minnesota

ART DIRECTOR/

DESIGNER: William Homan

172

Incentive campaign for

prospective home-buyers.

DESIGN FIRM: AD/Design,

New Milford, Connecticut

DESIGNER: Trisha Barry

ILLUSTRATOR:

Susan Martone

Problem #1

Your customers have found a
home they love at Sullivan Farm

. . .but their old house just isn't selling. . .

WE HAVE THEIR SOLUTION

Solution #1

The Guaranteed
Purchase Agreement

Sometimes selling a house is easy. Oftentimes it's not. We understand that carrying two mortgages is more than your customers can comfortably handle. Our Guaranteed Purchase Agreement is designed to help remove the two mortgage worry for qualified buyers at Sullivan Farm.

For a comprehensive explanation and a copy of the Guaranteed Purchase Agreement, please contact a Sullivan Farm sales counselor at 203/354-1914.

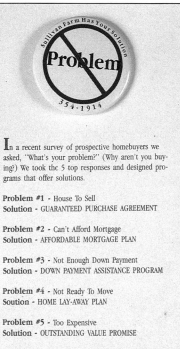

In a recent survey of prospective homebuyers we asked, "What's your problem?" (Why aren't you buying?) We took the 5 top responses and designed programs that offer solutions.

Problem #1 - House To Sell
Solution - GUARANTEED PURCHASE AGREEMENT

Problem #2 - Can't Afford Mortgage
Solution - AFFORDABLE MORTGAGE PLAN

Problem #3 - Not Enough Down Payment
Solution - DOWN PAYMENT ASSISTANCE PROGRAM

Problem #4 - Not Ready To Move
Soution - HOME LAY-AWAY PLAN

Problem #5 - Too Expensive
Solution - OUTSTANDING VALUE PROMISE

At Sullivan Farm we offer a number of incredible buyer assistance programs. If one of the problems listed above is keeping your customer from buying a home, talk to a Sullivan Farm sales counselor. We'll give you all the details on how we can help your customer buy a home at Sullivan Farm.

SULLIVAN
FARM

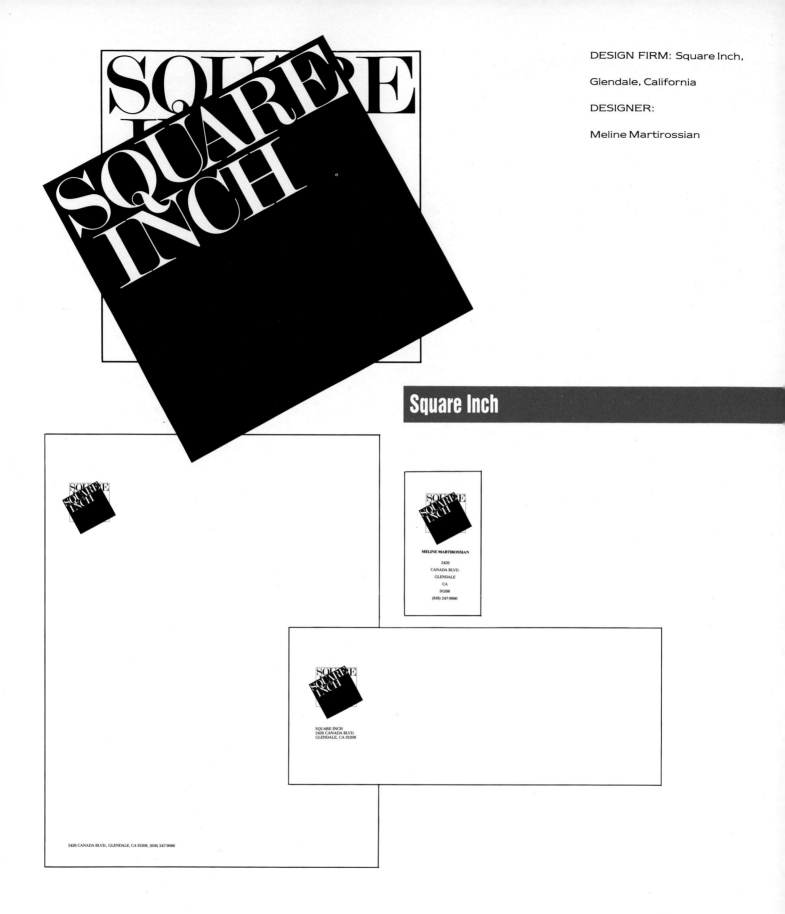

DESIGN FIRM: Square Inch,

Glendale, California

DESIGNER:

Meline Martirossian

Square Inch

MELINE MARTIROSSIAN

2426
CANADA BLVD.
GLENDALE
CA
91208
(818) 247-9986

SQUARE INCH
2426 CANADA BLVD.
GLENDALE, CA 91208

2426 CANADA BLVD., GLENDALE, CA 91208, (818) 247-9986

KATHRYN A. KELLEY

Computer business
systems developer and
planner.
DESIGN FIRM:
Bruce Yelaska Design,
San Francisco, California
DESIGNER: Bruce Yelaska

Kathryn A. Kelley

KATHRYN
A.
KELLEY
Business
Systems
Consulting

114 Sansome Street
Suite 1205
San Francisco
California 94104
415. 956. 5117

DESIGN FIRM:

Janson Communications/

Design, Coral Gables,

Florida

ART DIRECTOR/

ILLUSTRATOR:

Jeanne Janson

DESIGNER: Chik Shank

Acupuncture Center for Traditional Chinese Medicine

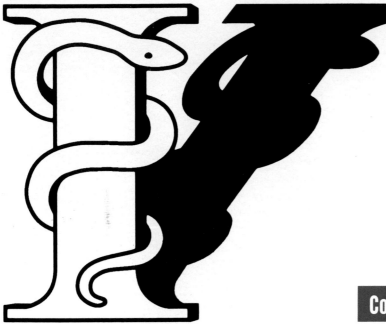

DESIGN FIRM:

Biomedical Communications

Center, Urbana, Illinois

DESIGNER:

Katherine Galasyn-Wright

College of Veterinary Medicine

University of Illinois
COLLEGE OF VETERINARY MEDICINE

177

THE
PALMS
AT WAILEA

DESIGN FIRM:

Clarence Lee Design,

Honolulu, Hawaii

ART DIRECTOR/

DESIGNER: Clarence Lee

DESIGNER: Eric Clegg

The Palms at Wailea (Hotel)

Lion & Lamb Development Inc.

Land development firm

owned by Mssrs. Lion and

Lamm.

DESIGNER:

Elizabeth Obernesser,

Stratford, Connecticut

AGENCY:

Kufeld Organization

Lion & Lamb
Development, Inc.

178

DESIGN FIRM:

Peterson & Company,

Dallas, Texas

DESIGNER:

Bryan L. Peterson

Margaret Watson Represents (Photographers Representative)

DESIGN FIRM:

Sue Lehmberg Graphic

Design, Monsey, New York

DESIGNER: Sue Lehmberg

SUE LEHMBERG
Graphic Design
192 Viola Road
Monsey, New York 10952
914 356 6533

Sue Lehmberg

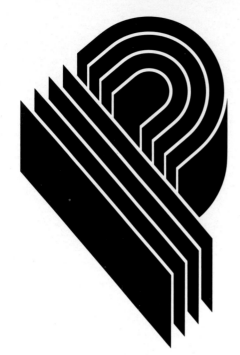

DESIGN FIRM: Murrie-

White Drummond Lienhart,

Chicago, Illinois

DESIGNER: Michael Kelly

LETTERING: Horst Mickler

PROTOTYPE
SERVICES
INCORPORATED

1660 NORTH BESLY COURT
CHICAGO IL 60622

PHONE 312 772 9200
FAX 312 772 7117

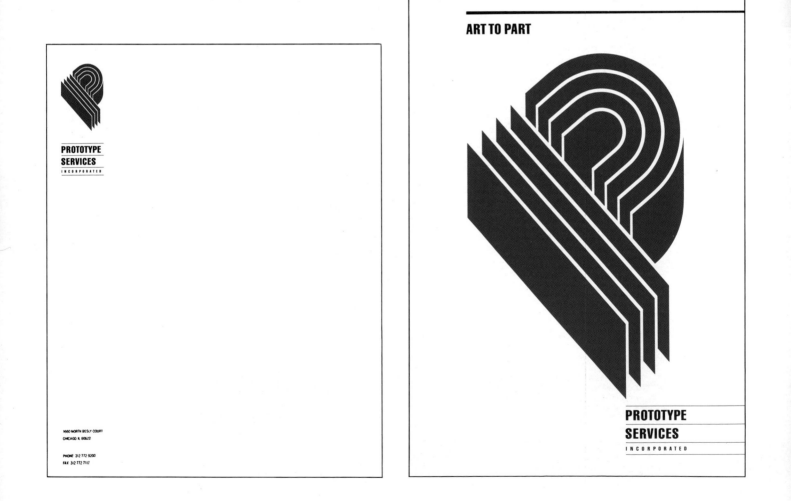

ART TO PART

PROTOTYPE
SERVICES
INCORPORATED

Manufacturer of industrial gears and bearings.

DESIGN FIRM:

John Leifer Ltd., Shawnee Mission, Kansas

ART DIRECTORS:

Garth T. Krizman, Kevin Venhaus

A SSOCIATED
B EARINGS
C OMPANY

ASSOCIATED BEARINGS COMPANY

GEORGE JOHNSON
Corporate Vice President
Sales

PHONE: 1-816-421-0407
IN-WATS: 1-800-888-5542
FAX NO.: 1-816-283-3287

2020 WYANDOTTE
P.O. BOX 412756
KANSAS CITY, MO
84141

Galbreath-Huff Companies (Real Estate Development)

DESIGN FIRM:

Rickabaugh Graphics, Gahanna, Ohio

ART DIRECTOR/ DESIGNER:

Eric Rickabaugh

CARETAKERS OF

GALBREATH·HUFF
PROPERTY
MANAGEMENT

EXCELLENCE

641 West Lake Street - Suite 501 - Chicago, IL 60661
Phone: 312-831-1200

Steele Design

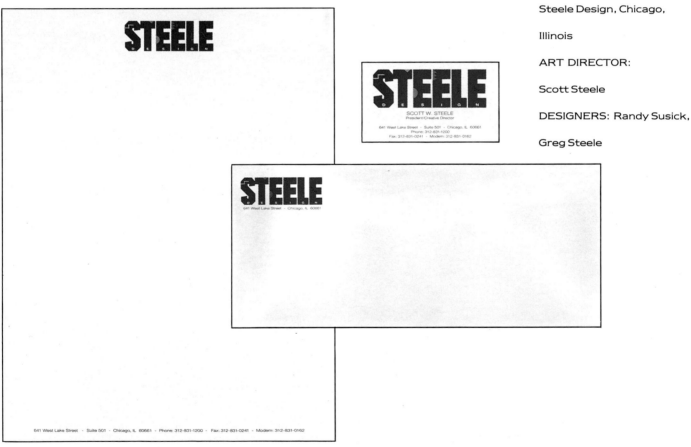

DESIGN FIRM:

Steele Design, Chicago,

Illinois

ART DIRECTOR:

Scott Steele

DESIGNERS: Randy Susick,

Greg Steele

A firm specializing in
marketing communications
for consumer products
aimed at women.
DESIGN FIRM:
Design Office of Emery/Poe,
San Francisco, California
ART DIRECTOR/
DESIGNER: David Poe
DESIGNER/ILLUSTRATOR:
Jonathan Mulcare

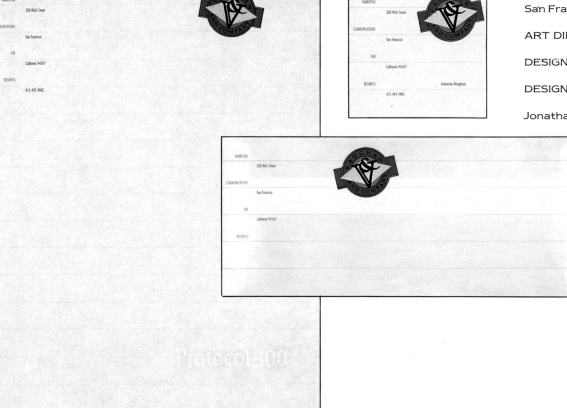

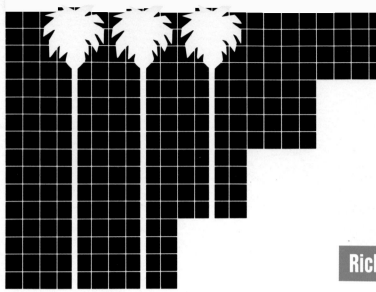

A Southern California

landscape architect.

DESIGN FIRM:

Sawcheese Studio, Santa

Monica, California

DESIGNER:

Sachi Kuwahara

Richard L. Segal & Associates

Upscale burger bar with a

tropical theme.

DESIGN FIRM:

Ken Shafer Design, Seattle,

Washington

DESIGNER: Ken Shafer

CLIENT:

Errol Dahl/Paradise Grill

Paradise Grill

DESIGN FIRM:

Lichtenstein Marketing

Communications,

Rochester, New York

DESIGNER:

Mark Lichtenstein

Alling & Cory Paper Company

Cafe Bistro

Restaurant in the Tai Ping

Yang Westin Hotel in

Shanghai.

DESIGN FIRM:

Pat Hansen Design, Seattle,

Washington

ART DIRECTOR/

DESIGNER: Pat Hansen

DESIGNER/ILLUSTRATOR:

Sheila Schimpf

CLIENT:

Westin Hotels and Resorts

185

DESIGN FIRM:

Gardner Greteman

Mikulecky, Wichita, Kansas

DESIGNER: Bill Gardner

Total Lawn Care, Inc.

DESIGN FIRM:

Gardner Greteman

Mikulecky, Wichita,

Kansas

DESIGNER: Bill Gardner

Wichita Cat Hospital

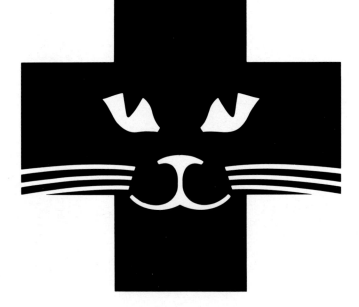

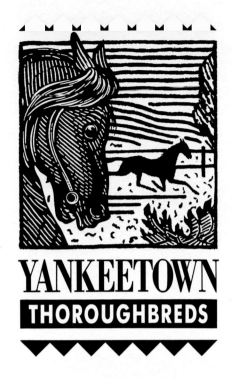

DESIGN FIRM:

Rickabaugh Graphics,

Gahanna, Ohio

ART DIRECTOR:

Eric Rickabaugh

DESIGNER: Mark Krumel

Yankeetown Thoroughbreds (Breeding Farm)

DESIGN FIRM:

Tackett-Barbaria Design,

Sacramento, California

ART DIRECTOR:

Kim Tackett

DESIGNER: Kyp Griffin

The Game Store

DESIGN FIRM:

Studio Rae+Caillet-Bois,

Glendale, California

ART DIRECTOR/

DESIGNER:

Ricardo Caillet-Bois

ILLUSTRATOR:

Sherry McKillop

Youth Theatre Northwest

DESIGN FIRM: Leslie Phinney

Phinney Design Inc.,   DESIGNER: Jini Choi

Seattle, Washington   ILLUSTRATOR:

ART DIRECTOR: Meredith Yasui

INDEX

ART DIRECTORS DESIGNERS

ILLUSTRATORS
PHOTOGRAPHERS
COPYWRITERS
CALLIGRAPHERS
TYPOGRAPHERS